An exercise in

UNDERSTANDING THE QUR'AN

An outline study of the last thirty Divine Discourses (*Sūrah* 85 – *Sūrah* 114)

Irfan Ahmad Khan

Foreword by

Mustansir Mir

ASSOCIATION FOR QUR'ANIC UNDERSTANDING

2nd Revised Edition 2013

ISBN: 978-1567447736

Published by:
The association for Quranic Understanding

Distributed by
Kazi Publicationjs
3023 West Belmont Avenue
Chicago, IL 60618
(T) 773-267-7001 (F) 773-267-7002

DEDICATED TO

The Prophet, peace be upon him, who received the final edition of the Revealed Guidance in Divine Words and explained it through his own words and deeds, i.e., his *Sunnah.* The Qur'an and the *Sunnah* will remain the source of guidance as the humankind continues its journey till the Last Day!

Contents

Foreword

Dr. Irfan Ahmad Khan passionately holds that readers of the Qur'an should strive to establish a personal relationship with the Qur'an—a relationship based on a direct understanding of the Islamic Scripture. In his view, a teacher of the Qur'an should attempt to help his students develop an independent understanding of the Qur'an, a task that Dr. Irfan Khan carefully distinguishes from that of a teacher presenting before his students his personal understanding of the Scripture. With this aim in mind, Dr. Irfan Khan engages in what he calls an exercise in understanding the Qur'an, the exercise consisting in a study of the last thirty surahs (chapters) of the Qur'an.

After discussing, in the Introduction, a series of definitional, textual, conceptual, and thematic issues—pertaining to the Qur'an in general, and to the surahs under study in particular—Dr. Irfan Khan offers a treatment of the chosen surahs one by one, in each case translating the surah, outlining the surah's structure, and offering brief notes on the interpretation of the surah.

In the last part of the book, he offers a general discussion of the surahs, dividing these into five categories and explaining the sequential relationship, first, between the surahs in each category and, then, between the categories themselves. These observations, which are suggestive as much as they are informative, provide a useful synoptic view of the thematic relationships marking an important segment of the Qur'anic text.

Mustansir Mir
Youngstown State University

Preface

In the Qur'an, it is God, The Lord of Humankind (1:1), Who is talking to God's servants. The Qur'an is an open book which invites every human to its reading (96:1,3). Listen to The Divine Speech (*KalāmAllāh*) attentively and seriously strive to understand it. Interpreters and commentators are teachers. As such they are welcome to help us. But they do not have to remain standing between God and God's servants. Let there be a direct communication between God and God's servants. No one has the ability to communicate the way God communicates. There has to be a listening to God, in which others are not permitted to distract (7:204). It is a right as well a duty of each believer!

Understanding the Qur'an is an ongoing process, initiated over fourteen centuries ago. The Prophet remarked: 'Its treasures/wonders will never be exhausted.' Contemporary readers who learn from earlier generations should keep moving forward, understanding the Text in changing human situations and with their growing abilities and skills. As the progress in human knowledge and understanding continues, so does our understanding of the Divine Text. The Prophet explained the Book through his words and deeds. He has indeed a very special status. Yet, he always emphasized that believers maintain their direct relationship with the Divine Book. He placed his own Sunnah next to it.

The believing as well as non-believing readers should keep in mind that the Qur'an presents itself as the last edition of the Divine Book, revealed to earlier messengers of The One God, sent in every corner of the civilized world.

If the believing community maintains its fresh touch with the Arabic Qur'an, the progress in human knowledge and technology should pave the way to a progressive and authentic understanding of the Qur'an_ which is our main concern. Keeping this in mind, our most pressing need is: Qur'anic teachers who will connect the believers directly to the Divine Text and cultivate in them ability and skill to undersand it afresh. We, therefore, underline the need for building such institutions as will prepare Quranic teachers qualified for this purpose.

Irfan Ahmad Khan
Association for Qur'anic Understanding
April 28, 2013

Chapter One

UNDERSTANDING THE QUR'AN
A Discussion of Some Issues of Basic Importance

1. 'Understanding the Qur'an' is different from 'Understanding an Understanding of the Qur'an'!

Do we actually understand the Qur'an when we think 'we understand the Qur'an'?

In the following pages, which contain an outline-study of the Qur'an from Sūrah al-Burūj (85) to Sūrah an-Nās (114), my interest basically lies in helping my readers in Understanding the Qur'anic text with their own minds. Delivering my own understanding of the Qur'an to the audience is not the purpose.

I underline the difference between 'a teacher's delivering his or her understanding of the Text to the students' and 'his or her helping these students understand the Text with their own minds.' According to me, it is only in the latter case that one is doing his or her duty as a teacher of the Text. And in this book I am trying to do my duty as a teacher of the Text.

What is important: The act of understanding a text by someone involves striving to develop an insight into its meanings through building one's own direct relationship with its verbal content. In the present case this text is a linguistic expression in the Arabic language.

However, I have observed that while serious students of the Divine Book are expected to keep their focus on the Divine Text, quite a few students show a tendency to lose this focus while receiving benefit from a teacher or a helping book. When they listen to an understanding of the Text by their teacher or read a commentary of the Text, a secondary text comes into existence and unconsciously they develop a tendency to make this secondary text their sole object of understanding. As soon as they would have grasped the meanings of this secondary text, they are fully (though falsely) satisfied that they have done their job of understanding the Text. They have this false satisfaction even when they have lost their direct connection with their real Text, and actually they did not make any effort to *understand the Text itself.* In such a case, the focus of their act of understanding remains an understanding of the Text by their teacher or commentator.

We are not against receiving an external help for a better understanding of the Divine Text. It will be very unfortunate for today's students of the Qur'an to deprive themselves of the great treasures of classical commentaries *(tafāsīr)* of the Qur'an. However, there is a difference between the teacher and the text. We must treat these great commentators of the Qur'an as our teachers, and while receiving benefits from their insights we should not remove our focus away from the Divine Text which they help us in understanding.

In the Qur'anic perspective, a believer's reading the Qur'an, as well as a believer's listening to another person's reading the Qur'an, is virtually his or her listening to what God is saying to the believer. As we know, even when the Divine address, in the Qur'anic text, is to some other persons, God wants the believer to listen to what God is saying. It is required that we listen to God with full attention and understand the Divine Speech (*KalāmAllāh*) afresh with an open heart and open mind (7:204).

Never deprive your faculty of understanding of God's beautiful speech, which is full of meanings. And remember: God will not appreciate if other people's understanding of the Divine Text is, all the time, standing between you and the Divine Speech, which God wants you to listen to with your own ears and understand with your own 'aql (faculty of Understanding). While it is interesting to learn how different people understand The Divine Speech, and while we appreciate various people's effort to help us understand The Divine Speech, it is quite obvious that no one possesses that ability to communicate with us which God possesses. Therefore, we request that you strive to build a direct relationship with the text afresh.

[Developing communication with God is a matter of personal experience. This is true in the case of prayer or *ṣalāh*, in which case, mostly, God is the listener, and it is true of our own listening to the Divine Speech (*KalāmAllāh*) - as in our reading of the Qur'an or someone else's reading of the Book to us. In the above discussion we only wanted to underline that, while for a believer who is developing his or her personal communication with God through the Qur'an, seeking external help is quite often both necessary and useful, seeking external help is also liable to spoil one's own personal and direct relationship with the Divine Speech.]

However, before we proceed further, we must understand that the Qur'an is not one long Divine discourse. Rather, it is composed of one hundred and fourteen *sūrahs* (speeches). Each of these *sūrah*s is a complete Divine discourse which has its own unique message and style.

In his/her Qur'anic study, the believing reader of the Divine Text proceeds *sūrah* by *sūrah*.

2. *SŪRAH* AND WHAT IS INVOLVED IN UNDERSTANDING IT?

As stated above, the Qur'anic Text consists of one hundred fourteen *sūrahs*. Through the following study, I am trying to help my readers in their understanding of the last thirty *sūrahs* of the Qur'an. These are relatively smaller Divine discourses that are placed at the end of the Divine Book.

There is a tendency among English translators of the Quran to translate the word *'sūrah'* as 'chapter'. This creates a great misunderstanding concerning the meaning of a most important Quranic term. A *sūrah* is more like a complete sermon or lecture or even a book or an essay, rather than a chapter of a book. A 'chapter' is a division of a book. It conveys a sense of incompleteness, while a *sūrah* is a complete discourse.

The Qur'an has given an open challenge to those who have any doubt concerning the Divine Authorship of the Book, to just try to compose one *sūrah* like the Qur'anic *sūrahs* (2: 23). This clearly shows that a *sūrah* is more than a bundle of some illuminating but scattered ideas - as an uninitiated reader is, quite often, inclined to think. *Every sūrah has its own unique style of elaborating its central theme* which runs like an invisible thread from the beginning of the *sūrah* to the end of the *sūrah.* In fact, it is the central theme of the *sūrah* which gives the *sūrah* its unity.

While striving to understand a Qur'anic *sūrah*, one should keep going through the whole *sūrah* repeatedly - doing what the Qur'an calls '*tadabbur'* or 'pondering over the verbal content of *sūrah* - till one is able to see clearly *how various themes of the sūrah are united, through this invisible thread, into a systematic whole.* Thus, according to us, understanding a *sūrah* involves one's developing an insight into the *sūrah* as a whole and only those who fully *comprehend the thematic structure of a sūrah,* understand the ***sūrah.***

3. *ĀYAH* AND UNDERSTANDING AN *ĀYAH?*

A Qur'anic sūrah is composed of verses which are called āyāt (singular āyah, i.e. a sign). An āyah is a point, which is marked in the Revealed Text as such, by the Divine Author.

As we explained above, a Qur'anic *sūrah* is a complete discourse. However, this discourse is composed of *clearly marked units*, that is, *āyāt* which are points that the Author makes during a *sūrah.* Thus *āyah* is an important Qur'anic unit and ***āyah*-consciousness** is a necessary condition for the understanding of a Qur'anic text. We do not deny that quite often an *āyah* itelf consists of numerous points, each of which has its own significance, see, for example, *Āyah of Dayn* (2: 282) or *Āyah of Kursi* (2:255). However, in such cases *āyah* consciousness demands that we should be able see the **one composite point** which these numerous points make.

An *āyah* is, by definition, something which *calls for its own understanding.* Thus in its very nature, an *āyah* is *something meaningful.* This is why the Qur'an speaks repeatedly of 'reflection *(tafakkur)* upon Divine signs (*āyāt*)', i.e., deliberating over their meanings.

Only when the meanings of all these points (*āyāt*), which compose a *sūrah,* have been investigated, a reader's striving to understand the discourse (*sūrah*) as a whole, would make sense.

Even in understanding a part of an *āyah,* we should give due consideration to its having that specific place in the *āyah* which it does occupy. We should understand how this part of *āyah* helps the *āyah* in making the point which it does make.

Āyah consciousness involves our understanding boundaries of individual *āyāt.* If we do not have a clear understanding about some individual *āyāt* concerning 'where does their linguistic expression start?' and 'where does it end?' then we are liable to miss something in the meanings of those *āyāt.* Likewise we can miss something in the meanings of any group of *āyāt* whose boundaries we do not understand very well. This will lead to a misunderstanding of the whole text and create confusion.

However, in the *understanding of an āyah* - over and above its own verbal content - the literary context of this *āyah*, and, therefore, its place in the *sūrah*, matters.

As we may explain later, meanings lie in the context. This is the reason why reciting the Qur'an over and over again or listening to its recitation is expected to yield better and better understanding of the Qur'anic Text. For example, in the first reading of a *sūrah* a preliminary understanding of the *āyāt* of the *sūrah* yields a preliminary understanding of the *sūrah* as a whole. However, in the second reading a better understanding of individual *āyāt* emerges in the perspective of a preliminary overall understanding of the *sūrah*, which is followed by a better overall understanding of the *sūrah* as a whole at the end of the second reading. Likewise, subsequent readings of the *sūrah* will further raise the quality of our understanding on *āyātic* as well as *sūratic* levels.

4. *ĀYĀT* AND THEMATIC STRUCTURES OF A *SŪRAH*

Thematic structure of a *sūrah* containing three *āyāt*

The smallest number of *āyāt* that a *sūrah* contains is three. This is the case with *sūrah al-'Aṣr* (103), *Sūrah al-Kawthar* (108) and S*ūrah An-Naṣr* (110). While these *sūrahs* are full of meanings, the understanding of their thematic structure is not problematic. One may try to see, for example, how the first *āyah* introduces the subject and how the second *āyah* proceeds further in that light. Hopefully, after taking these two initial steps, it will not be difficult to see, finally, the contribution of the concluding *āyah.*

Consider the case of *Sūrah al-'Aṣr.* It is the third *āyah* that contains the four-point formula which shows to humankind the way for the attainment of *Falāḥ* (Ultimate Success or Happiness). This is the *sūrah's* point of positive concern which it deals with at length. As we will explain in the Chapter on *Qasam,* the first *āyah* calls our attention to the Qur'anic review of the past history of human civilizations. Thus *qasam* in *āyah* (103:1) presents evidence from history to show how again and again the people who transgressed against God created corruption, oppression and injustice in human society. When they did not repent, in spite of the warnings of the prophets and messengers of God, they were punished and God wiped them off from the surface of the Earth. These corrupt and unjust people who had inherited the earth after the downfall of earlier civilizations, faced Divine punishment of humiliation in this life and in the Hereafter eternal punishment of Hell will be their share. In this light, the second *āyah,* which is concerned with the present situation of human society, observes: the way the people are conducting themselves today, it is very clear that the humanity is again proceeding towards self-destruction. Thus the *āyah* one and two together prepare the minds of the addressees for the understanding of the last *āyah* which contains the main point of Divine concern, i.e., 'how will humankind be saved?' The *sūrah* gives this question a positive twist: 'how will humans attain *Falāḥ?'* The reply to this question is elaborated in *āyah* (103:3).

Sūrah al-Kawthar (108): The first *āyah* introduces the Great Divine Gift to the Prophet whose blessings will go on increasing. The following *āyah* deals with the question 'therefore, what should the Prophet do?' The final *āyah* concludes: ultimately the crowd of those who are spreading hatred against you, will wither away.

Sūrah an-Naṣr (110) is mainly concerned with the question 'what the Prophet should do when the Divine Help and thereby Victory (110:1) arrives and this brings hosts of people into the fold of Islam (110:2)?' While the first two *āyahs* develop the question the detailed answer is summarised in the third *āyah* (110:3).

Structure of a small *sūrah* containing more than three *āyāt*:

To understand the thematic structure of other small *sūrahs,* the reader should consider the *sūrah* as a brief sermon containing three or more points – on the pattern of three or more paragraphs in a brief essay - and then try to see how these *āyāt* can be grouped accordingly. Each paragraph should have one *āyah* or more and an *āyah* should not be further broken.

(For illustration, please see in this book, our present exercises in unveiling the thematic structure of the remaining twenty seven *sūrahs.*)

Thematic structure of a large *sūrah*: *Sūrah al-Baqarah* (2).

Sūrah al-Baqarah (2) is the longest *sūrah* of the Qur'an. It contains two hundred and eighty six *āyāt*. It is much like a course of study. The first four *sūrahs* after *Sūrah al-Fātiḥah*, look like four courses of study for individuals belonging to the present community of believers. *Sūrah al-Baqarah* (2), which is the first course of study for the members of the Qur'anic Community, has four sections:

I. *Āyāt* 2: 1-39 address to human beings, in general

II *Āyāt* 2: 40-123 address to the Children of Israel

III *Āyāt* 2: 124-152 the legacy of Abraham: These *āyāt* connect the previous section to the following section.

IV *Āyāt* 2: 153-286 address to a New *Muslim Ummah*

In my 'Reflections on the Qur'an,' these sections are further divided into subsections.[1]

For example, Part I which is given the name 'To the Children of Adam' is divided into three subsections:

(a) 2: 1-20 studies three different attitudes towards the Book that help or hinder people's receiving guidance

(b) 2: 21-29 present the essential message of the Book

(c) 2: 30-39 deal with the story of of Adam & Eve and Divine Expectations with their children

Section (a) above (2:1-20) can be further analyzed as follows:

2: 1-5 those who will increase in guidance

2: 6-7 those who alreay rejected the invitation to believe

2: 8-20 those who are playing a double role

---

[1] *See: Irfan Ahmad Khan, Reflections on the Qur'an (Leicester, Islamic Foundation, 2005) pp. 53-59.*

Now it should not be difficult to see why according to us *Sūrah al-Baqarah* (2) is a course of study. Similar is the case with, *Āla 'Imrān*, *an-Nisā', al- Māidah* and some other large *sūrahs*.

Thematic structure of other *sūrahs:*

Our readers can imagine that the thematic structure of a medium size *sūrah* will have an in-between shape.

As we study a *sūrah*, the thematic relevance of its *āyāt* helps us in making paragraphs. Grouping the *āyāt* of a *sūrah* into paragraphs (or *rukū')* will helps us in seeing the overall structure of the *sūrah*.

5. THE ARRANGEMENT OF *SŪRAHS* IN THE QUR'AN

The order in which the Qur'anic *sūrahs* were sent down:

According to the Qur'an, in Divine creative activity (7: 54; 10: 3; 11: 7; 25: 59; 32: 4; 50: 38; 57: 4) as well as in Divine act of guiding, God chooses a step-by-step procedure. It is generally believed that the process of 'Qur'anic revelation' which started with the *āyāt* 96: 1-5, ended with '*al-yawma akmaltu lakum* .... .' in *āyah* (5: 3). Thus it extended over a period of twenty two years. *Sūrah al-Furqān* (25:32) explains that this gradual process was better suited to strengthenten the heart (and the mind) of the Prophet for understanding of the Divine Text – as was the case with slow and rhythmic recitation of the Qur'an. Whenever the time was ripe for the sending down (or *tanzīl,* i.e., revelation in installments) of a piece of the Qur'anic Text, to guide the Prophet and his believers in the concrete human situation that they were facing, God would select that relevant portion of the Divine Guidance, i.e., a *sūrah* or part of a *sūrah,* and reveal it to the Prophet. It was a gradual process of educating the believers through The Divine Text Book assigned to the community of the believers. It was expected that, under the leadership of the Prophet, the believing community, as a whole, as well as each of its individuals, will try to assimilate – both intellectually as well as spiritually - each new installment of Divine Guidance.

The order in which we recite the Qur'an today:

However, the officially appointed scribes of the Prophet were directed to place these separately revealed pieces of the Book according to the permanent system, as determined by the Divine Author, for all future generations. This was the order of the Qur'anic *sūrahs* in the Divine Book before its being revealed to the Prophet and this is the order in which the Global Muslim Community (*Ummah Muslimah*) reads the Book today. We believe that this systematic arrangement of one hundred fourteen Qur'anic *sūrahs* keeps their central themes in view. In the following we will have a brief look at the order in which the first nine *sūrahs*, which cover almost one third of the Book, have been arranged.

THE SYSTEM IN THE FIRST NINE *SŪRAHS*

Sūrah al-Fātiḥah (1): 'The Preface to the Divine Book'

Who will doubt that *Sūrah al-Fātiḥah* (1) is rightly placed in the very beginning of the Qur'an? In this *sūrah*, we praise the Merciful Lord of Humankind, Who is the Master of the Day of Judgment. We revive our covenant with God and pray for guidance. We pray that God helps us follow the path of the messeners of God and their blessed followers and that we do not follow the path of their unjust opponents who received Divine Anger. Through the following one hundred thirteen *sūrahs,* God answers our prayer.

However, after *Sūrah al-Fātiḥah* (1), we pass through three stages, before we have covered first one third of the Qur'an by the end of *Sūrah at-Tawbah* (9)

THE FIRST STAGE

The first stage deals with the Identity Consciousness of *this* newly formed community of believers and their relationship with others via *Sūrah al-Baqarah* (2), *Sūrah Āl 'Imrān* (3), *Sūrah an-Nisā' (4)* and *Sūrah al-Mā'idah* (5). These Four courses study a step-by-step growth & development of *Ummah Muslimah* in concrete life situations - as the process of Qur'anic guidance continues, in matters related with religion, ethics, law and governance.

Sūrah al-Baqarah (2) is very naturally the first course to be taught to the people who are born in believing families as well as those new-Muslims who join this community of *traditional* Muslims. This course of study is a Divine Gift to both of them. It contains both the philosophical basis as well as the historical foundation, required to strengthen and enrich their pride as a *Community of God's Obedient Servants*, *i.e.*, *Muslims*. As these traditional Muslims will contemplate the *āyāt* of *Sūrah al-Baqarah* (2), they will be slowly transformed into *real Muslims*, persons who have submitted to God, as God's obedient servants. Through this course of Qur'anic Study, they will understand the purpose of human creation and the Divine expectations from the present community of believers. The *sūrah* explains the meaning of 'being chosen' and the Divine expectations from those who are chosen, mainly in the context of the Children of Israel as well as the present believing community. This course studies, in a concrete perspective, basic principles of Islamic Ethics and Islamic Law and examines in detail problems that usually arise within believers' family life. *Al-Baqarah* gives to the Divine Text as a whole the status of a covenant between God and this newly borm believing community. At end the believers make *du'ā* (pray) that its fulfillment becomes easy for them.

Āla 'Imrān (3), which builds upon the above foundation, is the second course of study to be taught to the Children of the Muslim Community. The *āyāt* of *Sūrah Āla 'Imrān* make a *fresh* and more forceful restatement of the basic principles on which the Qur'anic Movement is based. It deals with some of those issues which were discussed in *al-Baqarah,* on a still higher intellectual, moral and spiritual plane. This brings conceptual clarity concerning issues of utmost importance for the future progress of Qur'anic Movement. However, all this is done in the concrete situation of conflict with the opponents of the Qur'anic Movement in general, and the People of the Book in particular.

In *al-Baqarah* the Children of Israel were reminded of the Divine expectations from them, and their actual performance was critically examined in the light of their covenant. In *Āla 'Imrān,* the focus turns on the life and mission of Jesus, and the Qur'anic Community initiates a dialogue with the Christians.

During the Makkan Period, the dominant forces inside and around the city considered the growth of the Qur'anic Movement a threat to their unjust system, and this is why they had been trying to silence this new voice which demanded a radical change in their corrupt ways of thinking and doing. During *al-Baqarah* Stage, which starts with believers' being settled in Madinah, their new Home of Peace, after their having successfully migrated from Makkah, these aggressors initiated military operations against the believing community. The believing community, which was, earlier, repeatedly advised to observe tolerance, forgiveness and non-violence - in spite of their right to retaliate - was now permitted to raise arms against these aggressors. *Sūrah al-Baqarah* justified, through rational arguments, why in the new situation created by these opponents of the Qur'anic Movement, this change in policy became essential. In view of the increasing enmity of these unjust opponents, *Sūrah Āla 'Imrān* makes the solidarity of the believing community its primary concern. It guides the believing community, at each step, during its clash with the outside enemies as well as the inside enemies. The latter were the people who apparently belonged to the believing community, but they were working as enemy agents.

However, *Sūrah an-Nisā'*(4), which is at this stage the third course of study for the believing community, represents the further progress of the Qur'anic Movement in its concrete perspective. It discusses almost all the issues, *Sūrah al-Baqarah* and *Sūrah Āl 'Imrān* dealt with, on a more advanced level. *Sūrah an-Nisā'* explicates the theological and ethical foundations of the social system which the Qur'an was buildings and further works out its practical details. Unlike *Āla 'Imrān, Sūrah an-Nisā'* also deals with Divine guidance in the domain of law, working out further details of those laws that were introduced in *Sūrah al-Baqarah* (2). *Sūrah an-Nisā'* (4) also guides the domain of governance and discipline. However, protection of the weak and marginalized sections of society remains its main concern in all these issues.

Sūrah an-Nisā' is followed by *Sūrah al-Mā'idah* (5), which is, at this stage, the concluding course of study for the Qur'anic Community. *Sūrah al-Mā'idah* (5), therefore, gives finishing touches to the matters that were discussed in the preceding three *sūrahs*, and this includes the domain of law. While reviewing the Divine blessings to the Qur'anic Community throug its development, the present believers are advised to learn lessons from the achievements as well as shortcomings of their predecessors who quite often failed to be truthful to their covenant.

THE SECOND STAGE

Sūrah al-An'ām (6) and *Sūrah al-A'rāf* (7) are the two following courses of study which introduce to the human world the Qur'anic message and the Qur'anic mission. Mainly the Qur'anic discussions in *Sūrah al-An'ām* (6) clarify the basic concepts of the Divine Book for the benefit of human beings in general. While *Sūrah al-A'rāf* (7) discusses the development of the prophetic movements as well as the place of the Qur'anic Movement in the perspective of the mission of humankind on Earth.

In the first stage, through the study of the above four *sūrahs,* the Qur'anic focus was on the solidarity of the Believing Community. These *sūrahs* dealt with a step by step process through which, in a concrete situation, the development of the first generation of this Believing Community took place. [As if they were born in Madinah and not in Makkah.] Now in the second stage, the focus is turned to the conceptual clarification of the *tawhīdic* message and the development of the *tawhīdic* movement in the perspective of the descend of the Children of Adam on Earth. Here also, *Sūrah al-An'ām* (6) lays down a foundation and the following higher course of study (i.e.) *Sūrah al-A'rāf (7),* builds further upon that foundation. When the Qur'an clarifies its basic concepts to the human world, the believing community receives all the educational benefits for its own intellectual, moral and spiritual development and growth and thus prepares itself for taking the Qur'anic message to the rest of humanity.

Due to the primacy of Qur'anic concern with humankind in general, one may consider that these two Divine discourses should have been placed before *al-Baqarah, Āla 'Imrān, an-Nisā'* and *al-Mā'idah.* Only when some humans have responded positively to the Qur'anic call and thereby a believing community has come into existence, it would be a right time for the sending down (*tanzīl)* of the *sūrahs* like *al-Baqarah, Āla 'Imrān, an-Nisā'* and *al-Mā'idah.*

This consideration was actually part of the Divine Policy concerning the chronology of revelation to the Prophet. We mean, historically *Sūrah al-An'ām* and *Sūrah al-'A'rāf* as well as other Makkan *sūrahs* were revealed to the Prophet before *al-Baqarah, Āla 'Imrān, an-Nisā', al-Mā'idah* and other *Madanī sūrahs.* However, now when a Qur'anic community is already in existence, the Divine Wisdom demands that this these people should first go through the above four courses of historical development to strengthen their own communal being before their encounter with the human world, under the guidance of *al-An'ām* and *al-'A'rāf.*

Given the reality that *Sūrah al-An'ām* (6) and *Sūrah al-A'rāf* (7) are two Qur'anic encounters with humanity in general, the question does arise: 'who will do this encounter?' I mean, 'where are the readers who will do the encounter on behalf of the Divine Book, and who should be educated through these two courses for this assignment from the Qur'anic Movement?' In the contemporary educational system one needs a bachelor degree before one qualifies for post graduate classes. It seems, in order to perform their educational role as two post-graduate courses of study , *Sūrah al-An'ām*(6) and *Sūrah al-A'rāf* (7), are looking for Qur'anic graduates who have already completed the study of *al-Baqarah, Āla 'Imrān*, *an-Nisā'* and *al-Mā'idah.*

A comprehensive study of these first four undergraduate courses in the Qur'anic Studies will prepare the Children of the Qur'anic Community to do the job of leading a Qur'anic Movement in the human world. These two new and higher courses of study are designed to cultivate among Qur'anic students quite a different frame of mind. Earlier, these believing students of the Qur'anic studies considered themselves as primarily members of a chosen community and their belonging to the human family or their being servants of God (*'ibād-Allāh*), in general, was not so important to them. Unfortunately, it was the case in spite of the repeated Qur'anic reminding that the believing community's being chosen is basicaly a responsibility from God which involves a duty toward servants of God, in general.

Through these two higher courses of study they would learn how to *transcend their communal being* - coming back to the level of *'ibādullāh* in general and becoming part of a wider human world. Now, in *Sūrah al-An'ām* (6) and *Sūrah al-A'rāf* (7), the focus is on learning 'how to share, with the human world outside their own (so called) chosen community, what they were so much proud of.'

THE THIRD STAGE

It is not difficult to see why the following two Divine discourses (i.e. *Sūrah al-Anfāl* and *Sūrah at-Tawbah*) have their place and time right after *Sūrah al-An'ām*(6) and *Sūrah al-A'rāf* (7). *Sūrah al-Anfāl* (8) and *Sūrah al-Tawbah* (9) together bring the Punishment of God to the criminals, and it is what *Sūrah al-An'ām* (6) and *Sūrah al-A'rāf* (7) have been repeatedly promising. However, from believers' perspective, it is only an occasion for their own *tazkiyah* (self-purification as well as their spiritual and moral development) and *tawbah* (returning to God in repentance). *Sūrah al-Anfāl*

(8) and *Sūrah al-Tawbah* (9) deal with how believers' truthfulness to their covenant is tested in panic and at the times of war.

THERE MUST BE A SYSTEM UNDERLYING THE REMAINING ONE HUNDRED FIVE QUR'ANIC *SŪRAHS.*

Through the above discussion, we made an attempt to work out, tentatively, an outline of the system that underlies the first one third of the Divine Book. Later, in the last chapter of this book, again we will have a brief review of the system that underlies the last thirty *sūrahs* of the Qur'an. But what about the system, if any, that underlies the remaining eighty four *sūrahs*? And what is important: does any system actually underly the 114 *sūrahs* of the Qur'an, as a whole?

We believe that all one hundred fourteen *sūrahs* of the Qur'an are arranged according to a systematic scheme. However, it is not possible for us to work out the details of that sytem. According to us, the *sūrahs* in the first one third of the Qur'an as well as the last thirty *sūrahs* of the Book appear to be systematically arranged because all the one hundred fourteen *sūrahs* of the Qur'an are arranged according to a system.

Chapter Two

SWEARING OR QASAM IN THE QUR'AN
In the Light of Swearing in *Sūrah*s 85-114

Swearing or *Qasam* is a linguistic tradition.

When we swear, we underline what we are swearing for. However, our swearing is more than inviting the attention of our addressee toward something. We swear when we want our audience to believe that whatever we are saying is true. We present our swearing as our witness to make people believe us – we use our *qasam* as a collateral. Likewise, we swear to assure our addressees that we are serious and sincere about something. The literary style in Qur'anic Arabic has in its perspective the above linguistic traditiosn in the human world. Quite often, the *āyāt* containing the swearing present a perspective, which makes the truth of the following *āyāt* evident. The swearing in the Qur'an prepares the minds of the readers for a better understanding of the point the Qur'an underlines through *qasam* which is stated in the following statement or statements and which is called 'respond to the swearing' (*jawab qasam*). Quite often, a common observation is presented as a witness for the truth of respond to the qasam (*jawab qasam).* Consider first three *āyāt* of *Sūrah al-Burūj* (85):

By the heaven which has watchtowers (or *burūj* to guard its security),[2]

By the Promised Day,

By a witness and what is witnessed.

The above swearing helps the *sūrah* in making its central point:

This universe is not a lawless kingdom where no punishment
would follow when you commit a heinous crime and run away.

To achieve this purpose the Qur'an suggests: Look above. Does the heaven not look like *a well-protected mansion?* And this is what the *qasam* in the *āyah* 85: 1 signifies.

---

[2] *Buruj* are watchtowers in a mansion or fort.
Here the heaven is seen as a well-protected mansion or fort.

However, there is some skepticism concerning the criminal acts of some unjust people which, apparently, go unpunished. The *sūrah* brings another *qasam* in *āyah* 85:2 to remove this misunderstanding:

God has *promised* that there will be a Day of Judgment.

The discussion continues in 85:3, where another *qasam* related with that day is brought:

Witnesses will be brought to make a just case against the criminals (who will be duly punished).

2. Now, let us consider *qasam* in *Sūrah at-Ṭāriq* (86). Have a look at our study of *Sūrah at-Ṭāriq* (86) in the following pages. Consider the interpretation and understanding of the three *āyāt* of *Sūrah at-Ṭāriq* (86: 1, 11, and 12) each of which contains a swearing. It is very unusual that two of these are inserted in the middle of the *sūrah;* however, these two also re-endorse the first swearing (86: 1) and re-emphasize its point in the middle of the *sūrah*. The three cases of *qasam* in these three *āyāt* testify the main theme of the *sūrah*, which is developed through a step-by-step process - from the beginning till the end of the *sūrah.*

3. The swearing in *Sūrah al-Fajr* (89) mentions blessed moments which are used for contemplation, for remembrance of God and for seeking God's forgiveness. These are the people who care for their spiritual and moral development or *tazkiyah*. These conscientious people understand that they have a duty from God, toward alienated and deprived sections of society. There are others who do not care for the remembrance of God. They are so lost in the pursuit of worldly pleasures that they neglect their moral and spiritual obligations. It is due to them that human society is filled with corruption, injustice and violence. When the unjust people do not correct themselves in spite of repeated warning, Punishment of God arrives. God gives them humiliation in this life and in the Hereafter.

The *sūrah* concludes: those who remember God, mainly those who devote (e.g.) the blessed moments mentioned in 89: 1-5 to the remembrance of God, will have inner peace even here in this life. What is important, in the eternal life after death, they will enter Paradise and enjoy company of all virtuous people, in the Vicinity of their Lord.

The *qasam* in *āyāt* 89: 1-5, prepares the mind for the above discussion which expands through the following *āyāt* (89: 6-30).

4. In *Sūrah al-Balad* (90), 90:1-3 is *qasam* and 90: 4 is *jawab qasam* or what this *qasam* underlines.

By their nature humans are very hard working and thus they are capable of delivering much good for themselves and the rest of the world. However, sometimes they strive very unwisely in the path of their own destruction.

The *sūrah* explains the point of wisdom missed by these people who would throw away their wealth on showy occasions. They neglect their duty to the downtrodden and alienated sections of society, which the Qur'an emphasizes. Instead of learning any lesson from the Qur'an, these people consider the Qur'anic Movement a threat to their unjust authority. They are hurting the Prophet even in this secure city of Makkah.

We hope it should not be difficult to see how the *qasam* in the first three *āyāt* is related with *jawab qasam.* And then how the *sūrah* succeeds in making its points in this perspective.

In spite of the fact that God has given them the ability to distinguish right from wrong and the ability to communicate and correct each other, these transgressors ***strive*** so hard in the path of their own destruction! For hard-working people the path of good and the path of evil are equally open. The first one leads to Paradise, and the second one leads to the Hellfire. The wise hard-working people join the Qur'anic Movement; the unwise people stand in an opposition to it.

5. In *Sūrah Ash-Shams* (91) and *Sūrah al-Layl* (92), 'Sun' symbolizes the Revealed Divine Guidance. The same metaphor continues even in *Sūrah Aḍ- Ḍuḥā* (93).

Consider *Sūrah Ash-Shams* (91). According to this *sūrah,* human beings are broadly divided into two categories:

(i) Those concerned with their self-purification, i.e., their moral and spiritual development (or *tazkiyah*), who are trying to develop an excellent moral character (91:9). These are the people who will attain Ultimate Happiness and Success (*al- Falāḥ*).

(ii) Those who neglect their self-purification, i.e., their moral and spiritual development. They would not care what rotten character they are developing within their own selves (91: 10). These people are doomed.

***The āyāt* 91: 1-8 present a perspective for a better understanding**

of 91: 9-10. Consider the following.

The first four *āyāt* (91:1-4) speak of Revealed Guidance. The *āyah* 91: 1 refers to Revealed Guidance *in Divine Words* (e.g. the Qur'an), unlike *āyah* 91:2 which refers to the Divine guidance as explained and interpreted in human words. The following *āyāt* (91: 3-4) deal with the response to the Divine Guidance. The *āyah* 91:3 deals with the people who responded positively. These are enlightened people, whose lives shine in the Light of God. The *āyah* 91:4 mentions those who remain deprived – who, rather, conceal the Guidance.

Āyah 91:5 presents wonders of the astronomical world as witness and *āyah* 91:6 deals with the earth, which is the abode for human beings. Together both *āyah*s are saying: this vast universe, with this tiny earth in it, which has been made suitable for human life, is a witness for what follows.

Āyah 91:7 and *āyah* 91:8 explains that the excellence of humankind lies in their being moral and spiritual agents.

Thus *āyāt* 91: 5-8 place the Revelation in the cosmic perspective and point to the great moral and spiritual potentials that humans possess.

6. *Sūrah al-Layl* (92) further explains the suggestion of the earlier *sūrah* that people behave like day and night, depending upon whether they take care of their spiritual and moral development (*tazkiyah*) or totally neglect it. This suggestion is repeated in 92: 1-2. The rest of the *sūrah* relates how actually the two characters behave and what is, in the long run, the fate of each of them.

However, 92: 3 introduces a parallel theme which also runs throughout the *sūrah*. There are pairs everywhere: God has created *this world* as well as *the Hereafter*. The journey of life continues from this world to the next world. In the earlier part of your journey you follow or fail to follow the Guidance.

In the later part of your life you meet the consequences: your journey in the Hereafter is full of blessings or it is full of suffering.

7. It is very easy to understand the swearing in *Sūrah Aḍ- Ḍuḥā* (91:3) in the perspective of *Sūrah Ash-Shams* (91) and *Sūrah al-Layl* (92). Through the Prophetic Mission, God has initiated a process of bringing light to the human world (93: 1) which is at present covered with darkness (93: 2).

The **first one third** of the *sūrah* makes the following point: God will see that the human world does not remain in misguidance. A process for its enlightenment, therefore, is already initiated (93: 1-2).

(Maybe, the Prophet is concerned because of an unusual delay in the coming of a fresh revelation. Some opponents of the Qur'anic Movement are, possibly, trying to create doubts that no more revelation will now be coming and that God is not very happy with the Prophet.)

The *sūrah* assures that the question of God's withdrawing God's favor from the Prophet does not arise. Rather, the Prophet will be granted more and more Divine Favor and Grace.

The second one third presents the evidence from Prophet's earlier life and the last one third suggests a plan of action for the future.

8. In *Sūrah at-Tīn* (95), the swearing in each of the first three *āyāt* points to a historical geography. As if the three *āyāt* affirm 'Look at the prophetic movements led by Jesus (95: 1), Moses (95: 2), and Abraham (95: 3), peace be upon all the prophets. The immediate reference is to the three places which were three centers for prophetic missions. The prophets were human beings. A study of these prophetic movements clearly shows that human beings have essentially a good nature. The lives of these messengers of God practically demonstrated *what a great potential for moral and spiritual progress humankind possesses*! But then this study also shows how far some corrupt human beings can go in their state of degeneration. In fact, the way the opponents of the prophets acted wickedly, and the way the believers maintained their virtuous conduct in a very rotten atmosphere, in spite of great difficulties in their way, clearly demonstrates that the Religion is true and there must be a Day of Judgment. There must be a day when the virtuous will be rewarded and the wrongdoers will be punished. (95:4-8)

Thus the points which the following part of the *sūrah* is making – which constitutes respond to the swearing (*jawab qasam*) - clearly follow if we contemplate over the the first three *āyāt* of the *sūrah*. The *sūrah* concludes: the people who are unable to see the above are, in fact, blind. They even do not see that God is the best of all the judges!

9. *Sūrah al-'Ādiyāt* (100) contains only one long *qasam* which is elaborated through first five *āyāt*, in a step-by-step process. The truth which is asserted in 100: 6 is, in fact, a self-evident truth. Human beings knows it very well. The following *āyah* says, 'human being himself is a witness!' (100: 7) However, the *āyāt* of *qasam* (100: 1-5) compare this ingratitude of human beings to God with the loyalty and gratitude of the horses to their masters.

[As if the *jawb qasam* is: shameless is this ingratitude of human beings].

10. The swearing in *Sūrah al-'Aṣr* (103: 1) refers to the Qur'anic review of the history of civilizations. It reminds us of the fate of those nations which were materially very advanced but due to their transgression they filled the earth with corruption and did not correct themselves in spite of the repeated warnings of the prophets of God. Consequently, the Punishment of God eliminated them from the surface of the earth. This story is repeatedly told in the Qur'an. In that light, the *sūrah* asserts that today also human beings are rushing toward their self-destruction. However, humankind has surely a bright future and people will attain *al-Falāḥ* (Salvation and Ultimate Success), if they learn the lesson the Qur'an is teaching. This lesson is given the form of a four-point formula for the attainment of *al-Falāḥ* for humanity (103: 3).

Chapter Three

IMPORTANT QUR'ANIC TERMS AND CONCEPTS
(as used in these thirty *sūrahs*)

1. *'Abd, 'Ibādah, Mukhliṣ, Ḥanīf, Shirk and Mushrik*

Human - God relationship is the most important Qur'anic concern. We are using 'servant - Lord' for Qur'anic use of '*abd - Rabb'* which is the only true way to designate 'human - God relationship'. The Religion is, basically, interested in straightening human beings' relationship[3]with God, as God's servants (*'ibād,* plural of '*abd*) alone. God alone is our Lord (*Rabb*) and we human beings are servants (*'ibād)* of none but One God alone.

[In the above, 'servant' is used as a substitute of ''*abd'* which is the original Qur'anic term. Thus we will use 'servant' as a Qur'anic term in English. As such it should not be confused with other usages of the same English word, e.g., in 'house-servant' or even in 'car- service' etc. Likewise, we will be using 'Lord' as a real substitute for '*Rabb'* which is the original Qur'anic term. By using 'Lord' or 'lord' as a Qur'anic term, we will be using this English word in a well-defined specific meaning which should not be confused with its other usages.]

In *Sūrah Al-Bayyinah* (98) 'being sincere (or being *mukhliṣ*) in the Religion or 'purifying the religion' means 'being *'abd* (servant) only of God' or 'having God alone as one's Lord (*Rabb*)'. When one fails to do so, one is committing *shirk.* One does so in all those cases where one is associating partner with God - giving some-one-else status of a god (*ilāh*). According to a *mushrik,* someone other than God also shares divinity with God, while God is the Only One Divine Being. *Mushrik* is the person who adopted *shirk* as his/her way of life and who

---

[3] It is important to note that 'human - human relationship' and 'human - thing relationship' also depends upon 'human - God relationship'. When 'human - God relationship' is distorted, the human life as a whole is corrupt.

In the above, 'thing' stands for beings whose status is lower than that of humans. 'Things are for human beings' while 'humans are not for things'.

thus failed to be a sincere servant of One God alone. According to the Qur'an a sincere believer in One God does not mix up impurities in human - God relationship. In explaining human - God relationship, *Sūrah al-Bayyinah* (98: 6) also underlines that God wants God's servants to be *ḥanīf*, that is, God wants undivided loyalty from God's servants (*ibād*).

[However, it seems to us that in the context of *Sūrah al-Bayyinah* which is dealing with three groups, i.e. believers, People of the Book and *Mushriks* "*Mushrik*" is more like a proper name for a specific group, i.e., Pagans of Makkah etc. For example, even if some People of the Book commit *shirk,* they will not be included in the group of *Mushrikīn.*]

Otherwise, in the light of the above, it should not be difficult to see that when *Sūrah Quraysh* (106) asserts "Therefore, Quraysh should worship (do '*ibādah* to) the Lord of this House (of God)," it means that the Quraysh must abandon all *shirk* and stand up with the *tawḥīdic* mission for which Abraham built this international center for the humankind.

Sūrah al-Kāfirūn (109), implicitly, affirms that religion is basically concerned with building relationship with one's deity. In the context of *Sūrah al-Kāfirūn* (109) it is implicit that the believers are persons who are worshippers of One God alone. *Sūrah al-Kāfirūn* which stands for freedom to believe or disbelieve a religion, also makes it clear that the believers are not supposed to have any compromise in the fundamentals of *tawhīdic* mission.

As a general rule, ***'ibādah* (worship or service) is what a servant (*'abd*) of God would do to God for the fulfillment of one's servitude (*'ubūdiyah*) to God**. For example: A servant of God expresses his/her devotion to God by repeating God's (Holy) name (i.e. doing God's remembrance or *dhikr*) or through bowing down or prostrating before God or praying or supplicating (making *du'ā*) to God or making a sacrifice to God. A pagan also can perform similar acts of worship to other than God.

However, in the Qur'an, *'ibādah* is used in a wider context to include whatever an *'abd* (servant) does, as God's obedient servant, with the intention to please God and in conformity with God's commanments. It may be a duty assigned from God or an additional good action, which is supposed to bring Divine pleasure. In fact, *the whole life of a servant of God is 'ibādah* – as long as one is conscious of being God's servant and is trying to seek God's pleasure, conducting in the human world the way God wants one to do, all the time having consciousness of God.

2. *Dhikr: Tasbīḥ, Ḥamd, Istighfār* and *Ṣalāh*

Dhikr[4] is a general term for 'remembrance of God'. However, the above Qur'anic terms are concerned with making *'dhikr',* what is sometimes called 'remembering the name of God', for example, through repeating God's name or even reciting the Qur'an. This *dhikr* is an activity which is different from *dhikr* as a state of mind. The latter is keeping or having remembrance of God, that is, being conscious of God's presence. We should never be forgetful of our Lord. We should try to remain conscious of his presence all the time. In fact, *having* remembrance of God in our heart is the essence of *'ibādah.*

In making *dhikr* you may choose to make *tasbīḥ*, i.e., say *'subḥanAllāh'* (or 'Glory be to God' – literally, meaning 'God is the only Being Who is free of all imperfections.' It is, perhaps, *the first proposition a servant of God asserts as he/she thinks of God.* When we see wonderful creations of God, we exclaim, 'Glory be to God!' or 'God is free of all imperfections!' It is apparently a negative assertion. However, our intention is to say something positive. But when we try, we find ourselves helpless. Whatever we say always falls short of God's beauty and goodness. So we just exclaim: 'God is free of all imperfections!' 'God is beyond our praise!' so to say, God transcends all our conceptions when we try to visualize God's greatness, beauty and goodness.

What is important, making of a dhikr, for example, saying of *'subḥānAllāh'* is not done by our vocal organs alone - it is done by our heart and by the whole of our being.

Likewise, you may choose to say *ḥamd* (praise by way of thanks) to God. The next proposition which occurs in our religious consciousness is *'alḥamdulillāh'* ('all praise is due to God!'). In fact, this is what we say by way of thanksgiving to God; when we think God has done all this for us, we immediately exclaim:

---

[4] For a detailed discussion on various measures of *dhikr*, see Irfan Ahmad Khan, *Reflections on the Qur'an* (Leicester, Islamic Foundation, 2005) p. 88-92.

Reciting the Qur'an or listening to its recitation and reflecting over Qur'anic *āyāt* will also be included in the category of *dhikrAllāh.*

'*alḥamdulillāh*!' As we know, the first *āyah* of the Qur'an says 'all praise is due to God, Who is Lord of all human beings[5].' (1:1). Here we are thanking God for God's favors to the human world of which we are a member, as if we are thanking God on behalf of our human family. However, thanksgiving is more than *saying* something with the feeling of gratitude. We also need to do something by way of thanksgiving.

Sūrah an-Naṣr (110) recommends that we combine the above two religious propositions to say, 'We glorify God and (we do so as) we praise God by way of thanksgiving,' which is very similar to, 'We thank God, as we glorify Him.'

Sūrah an-Naṣr (110) introduces another most impotant form of *dhikr* when it adds 'and seek God's forgiveness' (make *istighfār*). *Sūrah an-Naṣr* (110) adds 'Verily, God is Oft-Returning,'. That is, 'God accepts the repentance of His servants.' That is, when the servant returns to God – God also returns to His servant. In the above light, the *Sūrah An-Naṣr* (110) is recommending us to say, '*SubḥānAllāhi wa biḥamdihī astaghfirullāḥa wa atūbu ilayh.*' (I glorify God with His praise; I seek God's forgiveness and return to God). Thus *Sūrah an-Naṣr* (110) has suggested a compound form of *dhikr* – a remembrance formula which is composed of three or four elementary propositions for doing *dhikr*.

Ṣalāh* is the most important form of worship *('ibādah) which is translated as *namaz* in Urdu, Turkish, Persian and some other languages. In fact, it is the the highest and the most important form of *dhikr. Establishment of ṣalāh stands, symbolically, for making oneself servant of God throughout one's life.* It is avery rich and composite form of *dhikr* which is done by heart, in words through local organs, as well as by bodily movements. In making *ṣalāh,* one attends the presence of God, taking one's leave from the rest of the world – standing humbly before God, bowing down and prostating …all the time remembering God and thinking of God. And even before we start, we are required to check that not only our heart/intention, but also our body, clothes, place of worship is also pure and that we have performed our ablution properly….

[5] The literal translation is 'Lord of all the Worlds.' However, the grammar of the Arabic word for 'all the worlds' suggests that are worlds of human beings or even worlds of persons.

3. *Īmān and Kufr, Taṣdīq* and *Takdhīb:*

In the following we are trying to understand the above four terms in the perspective of the Qur'anic Movement.

***Īmān* (Belief):** The Qur'an is inviting the people to come out of the servitude of other than God and become *One Family of the servants of One God alone*. See, for example, 2: 21-22 and 4: 36. Also consider 2: 83 and 2: 256, which further explain the meaning of these *āyāt*. Now if a person says 'yes' to the Qur'anic call - makes *shahādah* (stands witnesses) that no one is worthy of worship but One God - and joins the community of believers, it is *īmān*, or believing.

Thus, in the light of the Qur'an, believing (or *īmān*) is positively *responding* to the call of God, which God is making through the Prophet (2: 186; 3:193).

Of course, *believing* involves that we understand the message of the call, agree with it and **commit** to it. This commitment involves our *testifying* to the above call. We do it by our heart and say it with our tongue. This commitment does include our belonging to, or our *becoming actually part of, the community of the believers*. Those who responded to the call of Muhammad, the Messenger of God (peace be upon him), organized themselves in the form of a community and are now calling the rest of the world to join them (41: 33). As we explained in the above, *the Qur'an itself is the call*. Consider *āyah* 2: 41 in which the Qur'an, which itself *testifies to the revealed truth, given to the Children of Israel,* is inviting the Children of Israel to join the Qur'anic Community.

The Messenger of God explains the above Divine Call in his own words and **strives (**makes *jihād***)** in the way of this call, through the human situation he faces. In this striving *(jihād)* all sincere believers are behind the Prophet. They all follow his guidance. Thus it should not be difficult to see why the Qur'an repeatedly uses *īmān* (believing) for *jihād* (striving) in the Way of God (57: 7-8 / 61: 10-11)

The Qur'an underlines that the members of the Community of Believers do *believe in God, angels of God, books of God, messengers of God* – without making any discrimination among them, i.e., believing in some and disbelieving in others (2: 285). They also *believe in their return* to God.

***Kufr* (disbelief):** On the other hand, if one rejects the Qur'anic call, the Prophet is making, one disbelieves, i.e., commits '*kufr.*' Thus, in its Qur'anic perspective, both *īmān* as well as *kufr* involve *one's taking a positive or a negative step in response to the call which the Qur'an is making.* Essentially, believing as well as disbelieving is an action (2:256) that a person's heart does.

(Sometimes the Qur'an gives a legal opinion (*fatwā*) about persons acting in a certain way, that they are, in fact, committing disbelief (*kufr)* – meaning *their action amounts to or is as evil as committing disbelief (kufr), i.*e., rejection of the Divine call, the prophets of God and the Divine Book have been making, e.g., consider 5: 17, 72, and 73. In fact, giving such a legal opinion (*fatwā)* amounts to expelling an individual from the Community of Believers.

Now it should be clear: 'Non-believer' is a totally mistaken translation of *'kāfir'*.

'Takdhīb' is accusing someone of lying or saying concerning something 'it is a lie.' You do not only say 'I do not agree with you' you say violently 'you are lying' and you stand in opposition to it. We do it when someone is really acting criminally, and as a conscientious person we see that it is our duty to stand against this lie. If someone *says to a truthful person who is working for a noble cause 'you are a liar!'* it is criminal! This is the crime some opponents of the Prophet commit.

Therefore, in the Qur'anic contexts, ***takdhīb*** is more than just a rejection *(kufr)* of the Qur'anic call. It is a *violent opposition* to the Qur'anic Movement.

***Taṣdīq* (testifying),** likewise, involves that you say, 'Yes, it is true' and stand in support of the mission.

Taṣdīq and *takdhīb* are two important Qur'anic terms. Consider *Sūrah al-Burūj (*85), where some people's *kufr* (disbelief) is turning into *takdhīb* and thus the situation is going from bad to worse. This state of affairs is inviting Divine Punishment. God can take action against them, the way God did with some earlier people.

For repeated occurrence of *takdhīb* consider *Sūrah Ash-Shams* (91), which points out that it is due to Thamud's transgression (*tughyān)* or rebellious tendency that these people committed *takdhīb*. For the meaning of *tughyān* see the following note. This tendency developed in them due to the neglect of their *tazkiyah*, i.e., their own self-purification or moral and spiritual development, as suggested by the preceding *āyāt*. When such a rotten leadership developed in this nation, they did not care in spite of the repeated warnings of their messenger. At the end, Punishment of God eliminated the whole nation.

For another repeated occurrence of *takdhīb*, consider *Sūrah al-Layl* (92). Consider the suggestion (see 92: 5-10) that those who care for their social obligations and have a responsible attitude in life will testify (do *taṣdīq) al-Ḥusnā*, i.e., the Qur'anic Message, which is all Good and Beautiful. On the other hand, selfish and socially irresponsible persons will stand against it (do *takdhīb*). The *āyah* 92:15 underlines that such wretched persons will enter into Hell.

Consider both *Sūrah at-Tīn* (95:7) and *Sūrah al-Mā'ūn* (107:1) where the locution ***'takdhīb bid-Dīn'*** is used to denote (violent) 'opposition to the Qur'anic Movement which is striving to revive the Religion.' After presenting all the evidence, *Sūrah at-Tīn* (95) wonders; 'What is now the justification for people who are accusing you (O Prophet) of lying - because of your standing with *Dīn?*'

The *Sūrah al-Mā'ūn* (107) on the other hand initiates its discussion with the remark: 'Did you notice, who are the persons who say that the Religion is all lie' i.e. who are doing *takdhīb bid-Dīn*? As though it is asking 'do you know: "who are the real opponents of the Religion?"' The *sūrah* explains that these are the same people who disrespect alienated and marginalized sections of human society and who are unconcerned with feeding the hungry.

4. What is *ad-Dīn?*

The Qur'an uses '*dīn*' for 'religion'.

The Qur'an uses 'the Religion' or '*ad-Dīn*' for the common core of the teachings of the prophets and messengers. Thus, while religions are many, the Religion is one. The Religion straightens *human - God relationship.* When human - God relationship is distorted, the human life as a whole become corrupt.

As we explain in the following section 'God creates as well as guides' is the most fundamental principle of the Religion. Equally significant is the Religious belief that ultimately good people will be rewarded and evil-doers will be punished in the second more enduring phase of life.. This is the reason how, in the Arabic language '*dīn*' also acquired a new meaning, i.e., that of '*reward or punishment, due on virtuous or evil deeds.*'

Sūrah al-Bayyinah (98) uses 'the religion of the straight (nature of human beings)' for 'the Religion'. The *Sūrah an-Naṣr* (110) calls it 'The Religion of God' because it calls all people to worship One God alone.

In *Sūrah al-Fātiḥah* (1), 'the Master of the Day of *ad-Dīn*' is mostly translated as 'the Master of the Day of Judgement'. According to us, this translation is permissible only if 'the Day of Judgement' is treated as the proper name in the English language for that day. Otherwise, 'the Master of the Day of *ad-Dīn*' means: 'Master of the Day of Reward and Punishment, due on our actions,' or even 'Master of the day when the most important religious truth would manifest itself, i.e., when the good people and the evil-doers are duly rewarded.'

5. Creation (*Khalq*), Governance (*'Amr*); Guidance (*Hudā/Hidāyah*) and Divine Planning (*Qadr*)

***Khalq and 'Amr*:** God is the Creator, Who has given every being its existence. And God alone is the Being Who manages the affairs of God's creation (7: 54). *'Amr* (Governance) stands for this *running of the affairs*. God alone is the Ruler, the Sovereign (Lord of the Throne or *Rabbul 'Arsh*).

'Not only *khalq*, *'amr* also belongs to God alone'.

The Qur'an also underlines that both creation (*khalq*) as well as guidance (*hudā or hidāyah*) belong to God (20: 50). Thus *hidāyah* (*hudā* or guidance) is a part of *'amr* (God's governing or running the affairs). Or one can say '*hidāyah* and *'amr* are the same'. In the latter case, we would say: God created sun and moon, various plants and animals and continues to guide (i.e. govern) the passage of their journey of life (36: 38-40).

Sūrah al-A'lā (87: 2-3) underlines that God creates perfectly i.e.. God gives all the finishing touches to the Divine activity related with the creation of an object.

Sūrah al-A'lā adds, **God *plans and then guides.*** This planning is called '***Qadr***'. ***As if God makes a blue print of what God is going to do.***

[Please note, in its meanings, the root *(q,d,r)* has two dimensions:

1. 'having power or ability to do something.' The Qur'an repeatedly mentions: 'God is *Qadīr* (*i.e.* God has power) over everything.'

2. 'forming estimates', 'having calculations' 'evaluating' or 'judging' something. The *āyah* 6: 91 remarks: 'those who say, 'God has not sent down anything' esteem not God the way God should be esteemed.' That is, holding the view that God will leave people without any Divine Guidance is, according to the Qur'an, an insolent belief.]

Please note the repeated occurrence of *'al-Qadr'* in *Sūrah al-Qadr* (97). This *sūrah* is concerned with *the blessed event of sending down the Qur'an - a very significant item in Divine Planning*. Consider the following:

God created human beings with immense possibilities of intellectual, moral and spiritual progress. God gave human beings the ability to make moral judgments. And God sent prophets and messengers according to a systematic planning. At the very end, God sent down the last edition of the Divine Book to the Final Messenger of God. Due to its importance in Divine Planning, the night when this very significant event occurred has been given the name '**The Night of *Qadr.***' Mainly, *Sūrah al-Qadr* has given it the status of a recurring event. The Night of *Qadr* still continues to occur every lunar year, when angels bring to the human world fresh blessings (*'amr*) of God to the Qur'anic Community.

Later, it is God Who has been guiding all the progress in art, literature, philosophy, science and technology. God continues to guide God's sincere servants in their efforts to authenticate their understanding of the Qur'an with their growing abilities and in changing human situations. No more any *waḥy* will be coming. Still the Qur'anic community's intellectual endeavors will keep unveiling immense treasures of meanings in the Divine Words – as the Prophet himself indicated. When put into practice these discoveries will open the doors of many blessings to the human world.

6. Self *(Nafs)* and Spirit *(Rūḥ)*

The Qur'an uses '*nafs*' for 'self' - designating a human being or a person. We know how living beings, i.e., beings on botanical or zoological level - are different from non-living beings. However, even all the beings, which we study in zoological sciences, do not possess the same higher form of life. Human beings in particular possess a form of life which is higher than that of (other) animals. It will be more in conformity with the Qur'anic classification not to treat human beings as a sub-class of animals; rather we should place human beings in a higher world of persons, with angels and jinn. Unlike animals, for this higher class of persons alone, religious beliefs which guide people's moral conduct, make sense. 'Persons' constitute a class that is higher and altogether different from that of animals.

God blew God's spirit (rūḥ) into the body of Adam (32: 9/15: 29/38: 72) to raise human beings to a higher level of existence – higher than that of animals which are also created from clay.

It is the addition of *rūḥ*, to a living body, which otherwise existed on the animal level, which would create this higher form of life that human beings possess. Take away the *rūḥ* from the human body and it will be an animal at par with other living beings at the zoological level. According to the Qur'an such a person is (spiritually) dead (6: 122).

However, *the Revelation of the Qur'an would revive such a (spiritually) dead person to this higher life again* – in case he/she has not totally lost one's potential to receive (the message of) life from the Divine Book.

In the light of the above explanation, it should be clear why ***'ar-Rūḥ '* is quite often used in the Qur'an for 'Revelation' to the prophets and messengers of God (16:2; 40: 15; 42: 52). For the same reason, *ar-Rūḥ* is also used for the archangel Gabriel, who brought the Revelation (19: 17; 78: 38; 97: 4).**

7. *Taswiyah & Tazkiyah* of *Nafs, 'Itmi'nān* of *Nafs*

The above three terms belong to three very different domains. *Taswiyah* of *nafs* is related with Divine Creative Activity. *Tazkiyah* of *nafs* is an educational function related with spiritual and moral domain. And *'Itmi'nān of nafs* is a psychological state or function which is related with intellectual or spiritual achievements.

Sūrah al-A'lā (87:2-3) mentions the general truth: whatever God created, God perfected it - gave it all the finishing touches - and as a general rule, God plans and then guides. However, *Sūrah ash-Shams* (91: 7-8), specifically mentions:

Taswiyah* (perfecting) of *Nafs or God's giving finishing touches to God's creative activity related with a self and suggests that God's granting moral consciousness to human beings is part of God's giving human self (*nafs*) its perfection. *Sūrah as-Sajdah* (32: 9) explains that God's blowing God's Spirit (*Rūḥ*) into the human body helped the perfecting (*taswiyah*) of the human self (*nafs*). It gave us the ability to listen to Divine signs (*āyāt*), see Divine signs and reflect upon Divine signs.

Tazkiyah is, on the otherhand spiritual and moral development of one's own self (nafs). It denotes taking care of one's own self-purification and spiritual growth. Consider how the *sūrahs* 87, 91 and 92 deal with *tazkiyah.* The *Sūrah al-Fajr* (89) deals with *tazkiyah* at length without using the term *'tazkiyah'.* *Sūrah al-Bayyinah* (98) uses the term '*zakāh'* which is spending one's wealth in order to achieve self-purification. *Tazkiyah* is also mentioned in *sūrah* 79 and *sūrah* 80, which are not included in the present study of Qur'anic *sūrahs.*

At four places in the Qur'an, God mentions that the Prophet, who recites the Qur'anic verses to his believers, performs a number of educational functions. Among these, taking care of the spiritual development (*tazkiyah)* of his believers has a special place (2: 129 / 2: 159 / 3: 164 / 62: 2).

'Itmi'nān* of *Nafs (a person's being fully satisfied and having thereby perfect inner peace)**:** The *Sūrah al-Fajr* (89) concludes (89: 27-30) with the Divine address to the fully satisfied person **(*an-nafsul mutma'innah*)** who enjoys perfect inner peace and satisfaction**.**This is the person who made the best use of those calm and quiet moments which are mentioned in 89: 1-4 for the remembrance of God and for pondering over Divine *āyāt.* Throughout his life, he had inner satisfaction and peace of mind unlike the people mentioned in 89: 6-12. On the Day of Judgment also, this person has peace of mind and is fully satisfied with his performance in this life as well as with the Divine reward to him. He is pleased with God and God is pleased with him.

(For the meaning of the word ' *'itmi'nān',* we recommend that our readers have a look at *āyāt* 22: 11 / 4: 103 / 10:7 / 16:106.)

Sūrah ar-Ra'd (13: 28) mentions *'itmi'nān* of *qalb*' (satisfaction of heart/mind). In the first part of 13: 27 people were, in fact, demanding such a miracle which will make them sure (and thereby fully satisfied) that the Qur'an is from God. The second part of the *āyah* states priciple related with guidance. *Sūrah ar-Ra'd*

(13: 28) then underlines that those 'who believe and thereby derive inner satisfaction through remembrance of God (in this context, from listening to the Qur'anic *āyāt*) receive guidance from God. The *āyah* concludes: it is only through remembrance of God that '*itmi'nān* of *qalb* (satisfaction of the heart) is acquired.' That is, the fullest inner satisfaction only come from the Qur'an (which is a remembrance of God).

However, as 13: 27 had underlined, it is the story of God's submissive servants – those who turn to God. When *they* listen to the Qur'an truth becomes clear to them and their hearts/minds are fully satisfid.

In *Sūrah al-Baqarah* (2:260) Abraham is looking for the satisfaction of his heart/mind, and presents his problem to God[6]. Apparently, Abraham is facing a philosophical problem, which is resolved by Divine response. I mean, Abraham is actually seeking an intellectual satisfaction and not **satisfaction of heart,** as understood in its narrow sense.

(However, one can still argue that the solution of Abraham's intellectual problem will bring more of inner peace and satisfaction of heart to Abraham. But that is a different issue.)

It is interesting to note that in the above two cases, instead *of 'itmi'nān an-nafs'* (a person's inner peace and satisfaction) the word *'itmi'nān al-qalb'* or satisfaction of heart is used.

8. *Tughyān, Fasād, Fitnah, 'Amal Ṣāliḥ*

***Tughyān* (Transgression):** *Tughyān* stands for rebellious attitude in human - God relation. It is exceeding one's limits. It involves arrogance and lack of submission. It is one's failure to conduct as a servant of God.

We are one family of the servants of One God Who is Lord of all human beings. Members of this family are mutually concerned. They have mutual respect and share their resources with each other. God has assigned mutual duties. It is the right (*ḥaq*) of the down-trodden and alienated people that those servants of God who are well-off should honor them and care for them. They should help them

[6] For more details, please consider, Irfan Ahmad Khan, *Reflections of the Qur'an* (Leicester, Islamic Foundation, 2005) p. 690.

improve their condition. Likewise, neighbors and relatives have their rights and they should mutually share their resources.

***Fasād* (corruption) in human society:** The Qur'an underlines that corruption (*fasād)* in human life occurs when the people do not care for their social obligations, i.e. the duties assigned to them from the Lord of humankind. This would explain the nature of **relationship between transgression *(tughyān)* and corruption (*fasād*).** According to *Sūrah al-Fajr* (89: 11-12), it is people's transgression against God which makes them neglect their mutual duties and leads to corruption in the human world.

'Amal Ṣāliḥ (righteous action): If we understand, that *ṣālīḥ* is antonym of *fāsid* (corrupt), it will not be difficult to see why a righteous action is called ***'amal ṣāliḥ.*** The Qur'anic Movement is calling the people to stop their transgression against God, which has created corruption in the human society. When people will start caring for each other, doing their mutual duties, it will counteract the prevailing corruption in society and create a state of **reform** (***iṣlāḥ),*** as the Qur'an calls it. This is why at many places in the Qur'an the prophetic movement is introduced as a 'movement for *iṣlāḥ.'* The prophets of God were striving to *set things right* at a time when society was full of mischief, corruption and injustice. Consider, e.g., *Sūrah al-A'rāf* (7: 35, 56, 85, 142, and 170) to see how, again and again, God had been sending the prophets one after another when the society got filled with corruption (*fasād)* after the reform (*iṣlāḥ*) by the earlier prophetic movement.

Fitnah: However, when the above movement for *iṣlāḥ* (reform) is raised, **the transgressors try to meddle with it (22: 52-53),** giving believers a hard time or using diplomacy to achieve their goals.They may try to totally crush this movement for *iṣlāḥ.* They even burn the believers alive, as in *Sūrah al-Burūj* (85: 4-10). The forces of evil sometimes work from within the community of believers to corrupt this movement of reform (*iṣlāḥ*) from inside and distort its message. They may try to create differences and divisions within the believing community - creating confusions concerning its mission. All this creates severe *test situation* for the believing community and is, therefore, called *fitnah.*

The believers are advised to seek God's refuge from Satan, who plays with their sentiments and wants them to act fanatically so that it is easy to arouse other people's senti,ents against them. In order to eliminate *fitnah*, wisdom is required.

If you wrestle with it, you may flare it up and lose the battle. The Qur'an emphasizes returning good in response to evil (13: 22 / 28: 54-55 / 41: 34 / 25: 63). The believers, who keep remembering God and keep seeking God's forgiveness, are blessed with *sakīnah* (inner peace) which is, according to the Qur'an, key to victory (48: 4, 18, 26).

9. *Yatīm* (Orphan), *Miskīn* (Poor) and *Raqabah* (Neck of a Slave or a Prisoner)

***Yatīm* (orphan):** When the Qur'an emphasizes that we **honor orphan**, the purpose is to respect all the alienated or marginalized sections of our society.

***Miskīn* (poor):** Likewise, the Qur'anic concern with the poor aims at minimizing the gap between those who have and those who do not have.

***Raqabah* literally means neck: freeing a neck means freeing *a* slave or a prisoner:** According to the Qur'an all human beings deserve freedom. If some people have been unjustly captivated or turned into slaves, it is our duty to work for their freedom. Consider how *Sūrah al-Balad* (90), which underlines a few virtuous actions, gives priority to 'freeing the slaves.'

The above can be extended to helping all those individuals and groups whose freedom has been unjustly restricted. We can extend it to include financial slavery, which very often paralyzes the freedom of individuals and groups. Otherwise, the Qur'an uses '***ghārimīn***' for financial slavery.

10. *Taqwā* (Piety) and *'Istighnā* (Being free of any obligation/Carelessness)*; Taqwā and Fujūr* (Lewdness)*; Atqā* (Most Pious) and *Ashqā* (Most Hapless Wretch);

In this note, we will study *'Taqwā'* and its three antonyms used wihin these thirty sūrahs.

The first antonym is *'istighnā'*. While *'taqwā'* stands for 'a responsible attitude in life, *'istighnā'* signifies 'feeling no need to be concened with one's responsibilities.'

Muttaqīs (or the people who observe *taqwā*) are those who fear God and who are concerned that they should not fail to do their duty to God or his servants, as assigned by God. However, *Sūrah al-Layl* mentions (92: 5 and 8), there are, basically, two attitudes in social life. Some people share in the needs of others and maintain a responsible conduct throughout their lives. There are others who do not care. They have ***istighnā, i.e,*** they are carefree. They do *not* feel any need to be concerned with their duties. They do not think they have any.

The Qur'an also uses *fujūr* (lewdness) as an antonym of *taqwā*. According to *Sūrah ash-Shams* (91:8), God has inspired human beings with moral consciousness. Human beings can distinguish a licentious behavior from a conscienscious behavior.

However, 92:15 underline the contrast of *atqā* (most pious) *with ashqā (*most hapless wretch) - one who has become so stone- hearted due to his/her morally and spiritually corrupt behavior that the Qur'anic reminding by the Prophet (87: 9-11) does not do any benefit to him/her and he/she violently rejects the most virtuous message of the Qur'an (92: 9).

11. *Falāḥ* and *Khusrān*

'Salvation,', *'mukti'* or *'moksha'* and such other terms are used in religious literature to designate ultimate happiness or ultimate success in the eternal life, as a result of the pious and virtuous life in this world. The Qur'an introduces the word *'al-Falāḥ '* for Ultimate Success or Happiness, at the very beginning of *Sūrah al-Baqarah* (2:5). The same is repeated at the end of *Sūrah Al 'Imrān* in (3: 200). The *Sūrah al-Mu'minūn* (23) relates the qualities of the believers who will achieve *al-Falāḥ*. (23:1-11), and then affirms that *al-Falāḥ* lies in the inheritance of Paradise. *Sūrah Tāhā* (20: 118-119), suggests that in the Garden (*al-Jannah*) there is complete freedom from all kinds of pain and suffering. *Sūrah al-Baqarah* (2) makes it clear that the ultimate abode of God's faithful servants is a place where there **is no fear, no sorrow or grief, and no worries.** This theme is repeated in *al-Baqarah* six times.

Unlike Khusrān, Falāḥ is a positive concept. Faithful servants' return to **God's Garden** is their entering into the company of all the pious people (89: 28-30). They will be in the close neighborhood of God (54: 54-55). This brings immense aesthetic and spiritual pleasure (83: 23, 35 / 75: 23).

Sūrah al-A'lā (87:14) proclaims: the person who takes care of one's own *tazkiyah* achieves *Falāḥ*. *Sūrah Ash-Shams* (91: 9-10) states the same truth and adds: one who neglects one's self is ruined ('*khāba'*).

Sūrah al-'Aṣr* (103) which has 'path to *Falāḥ*' as its central theme** does not use the word '*Falāḥ*'. Rather, it makes an explicit warning that unless the humanity changes its path it is proceeding toward doom or total loss (Khusr***).

(The following two notes deal with four common words of Arabic language which are used by the Divine Text in a very meaningful style that is important for the students of the Qur'an to understand. These are not Qur'anic terms.)

12. *Al-Insān (the Human)* and *An-Nās (the People)*

Al-Insān, in its dictionary meanings, stands for humankind. However, quite often the Qur'an uses *'al-insān'* to denote 'the dominant current in today's human world.' It is a **literary style**. For example, consider 89:15, which criticizes *the way human beings are mostly conducting themselves today.* Obviously, there are exceptions to what is stated in 89:15 and the following ā*yāt*. This description of human conduct continues from 89:15 to 89:20. Then in 89: 21-24 a scene from the Hereafter is presented. Occurrence of '*al-insān'* is again repeated in 89:23. If you understand the ā*yah* in isolation, you will say, here it can be very well understood in its original meaning - denoting the whole species of human beings. But it is not a good idea to neglect the literary context in which the human society was being criticized for going the wrong way and its people would not listen to the Qur'anic remindig. It is the same *insān* - a representative of the same rotten society - who immediately gets the reminded when Hell is brought on the Day of Judgment (89:23).

However, in the present selection of Qur'anic *sūrahs*, *Sūrah al-'Alaq* (96) is the most important *sūrah* to understand Qur'anic usage of *al-insān*. Consider the first two occurrences in 96:2 and 96:5. *The first five āyāt are talking about human species.* The Prophet is being taught the Book, to read it to humankind. God, who created human beings out of clot, is teaching human beings – through the Qur'an – what human beings could have never known without Revelation. However, when you consider the third occurrence of '*al-insān'* (96:6), it is very clear that here the target of the Qur'anic criticism is the human society which the Qur'an criticizes. This society as a whole is acting as a transgressor against God. *Al-insān* is its representative.

Also consider *Sūrah at-Tīn* (95).

Áyah 95: 4 points to the *goodness of human nature.* Human beings are born with the most excellent potential - morally and spiritually. Here, there is no problem with the original meaning of *al-insān*. But then, what does '*al-insān'* denote when the Qur'an mentions *al-insān's* being degenerated to the lowest of the low in 95: 5. Consider 'him,' which goes back to *al-insān*. Obviously, the *Qur'an* is attacking the dominant current in the human society, which is conducting itself like beasts or even worse. Consider *āyah* 95: 6, which would highlight the blessed part of human species which was excluded when '*al-insān'* denoted only the dominant current of human society.

Now consider the occurrence of '*al-insān'* in *Sūrah al-'Aṣr* (103).

It should be obvious that although in *Sūrah al-'Aṣr* the Qur'an, apparently, affirms that humankind is at a loss, it only means that the way most people are behaving is leading them to loss.

We hope now that our readers will not have any problems in Understanding the Qur'anic complaint in *Sūrah al-'ādiyāt* (100: 6). The *sūrah* is, in fact, saying that *most human beings today are acting ungratefully*. The literary style to say this is: 'Surely human being (*al-insān*) is ungrateful to his Lord.'

An-Nās: 'The people' is a very good translation of '*an-nās*.' The Qur'an is **not** concerned with any **special section** of human society. It is concerned with all members of human society. It is concerned with human beings in general, though quite often it may have to address special groups.

God wants to speak to the masses and to the common men.

Consider 7: 158, where it becomes clear that all human beings are the addressees of the Prophet. Consider also 2: 21-22. This is the first occasion when the Qur'an gives its essential message. It is very meaningful that before addressing the believers (2: 104), the Children of Israel (2: 40), or the People of the Book (3: 64)), the Qur'an addresses humankind (2: 21-22).

[Consider how earlier prophets in *Sūrah al-A'rāf* {7: 59, 65, 73, 80, and 85} and *Sūrah Yūnus* (10: 71 and 84) use the address, 'O my people' {or *Ya Qawmi!*}. Also notice, the Qur'an sometimes introduces a prophet as their people's brother {7: 65, 73 and 85}. The purpose is to underline the feeling of brotherhood which they all shared with their people. This also confirms that the prophets of God address people in general and not any special group.]

13. *Al-Kitāb* (The Book) and *al-Qur'ān* (The Reader)

In this selection of the Qur'anic *sūrahs*, we have three occurrences of '*al-Kitāb*,' (the Book), all in *Sūrah al-Bayyinah* (98), and there is no occurrence of '*al-Qur'ān'* (the Qur'an). However, there is one occurrence of 'a *qur'an*' in 85: 21.

It is very interesting to note that the Qur'an uses '*al-Kitāb*' (the Book, in singular), for Torah as well as for the Qur'an itself - as if The Qur'an is a different edition of the same Divine Book.

There are a very large number of occurrences of '*al-Kitāb*' (the Book) in the Qur'an. Only three times (2: 285 / 4: 136 / 66: 12), the Qur'an uses *kutub* or books (in plural) for revealed books. The purpose is to underline many different occurrences of the revelation to different messengers.

Chapter Four

STUDY OF SŪRAH AL-BURŪJ

85 (a) Sūrah al-Burūj

سُوْرَةُ الْبُرُوْجِ

بِسْمِ اللّٰهِ الرَّحْمٰنِ الرَّحِيْمِ

وَالسَّمَآءِ ذَاتِ الْبُرُوْجِ ۝١ وَالْيَوْمِ الْمَوْعُوْدِ ۝٢ وَشَاهِدٍ وَّمَشْهُوْدٍ ۝٣
قُتِلَ اَصْحٰبُ الْاُخْدُوْدِ ۝٤ النَّارِ ذَاتِ الْوَقُوْدِ ۝٥ اِذْ هُمْ عَلَيْهَا قُعُوْدٌ ۝٦ وَّ
هُمْ عَلٰى مَا يَفْعَلُوْنَ بِالْمُؤْمِنِيْنَ شُهُوْدٌ ۝٧ وَمَا نَقَمُوْا مِنْهُمْ اِلَّآ اَنْ
يُّؤْمِنُوْا بِاللّٰهِ الْعَزِيْزِ الْحَمِيْدِ ۝٨ الَّذِيْ لَهٗ مُلْكُ السَّمٰوٰتِ وَالْاَرْضِ وَ
اللّٰهُ عَلٰى كُلِّ شَيْءٍ شَهِيْدٌ ۝٩ اِنَّ الَّذِيْنَ فَتَنُوا الْمُؤْمِنِيْنَ وَالْمُؤْمِنٰتِ ثُمَّ
لَمْ يَتُوْبُوْا فَلَهُمْ عَذَابُ جَهَنَّمَ وَلَهُمْ عَذَابُ الْحَرِيْقِ ۝١٠ اِنَّ الَّذِيْنَ
اٰمَنُوْا وَعَمِلُوا الصّٰلِحٰتِ لَهُمْ جَنّٰتٌ تَجْرِيْ مِنْ تَحْتِهَا الْاَنْهٰرُ ذٰلِكَ
الْفَوْزُ الْكَبِيْرُ ۝١١ اِنَّ بَطْشَ رَبِّكَ لَشَدِيْدٌ ۝١٢ اِنَّهٗ هُوَ يُبْدِئُ وَيُعِيْدُ ۝١٣ وَ
هُوَ الْغَفُوْرُ الْوَدُوْدُ ۝١٤ ذُو الْعَرْشِ الْمَجِيْدُ ۝١٥ فَعَّالٌ لِّمَا يُرِيْدُ ۝١٦ هَلْ
اَتٰىكَ حَدِيْثُ الْجُنُوْدِ ۝١٧ فِرْعَوْنَ وَثَمُوْدَ ۝١٨ بَلِ الَّذِيْنَ كَفَرُوْا فِيْ
تَكْذِيْبٍ ۝١٩ وَّاللّٰهُ مِنْ وَّرَآئِهِمْ مُّحِيْطٌ ۝٢٠ بَلْ هُوَ قُرْاٰنٌ مَّجِيْدٌ ۝٢١ فِيْ لَوْحٍ
مَّحْفُوْظٍ ۝٢٢

85 (b) Sūrah al-Burūj

وَالسَّمَآءِ ذَاتِ الْبُرُوْجِ ﴿١﴾

الْبُرُوْجِ	ذَاتِ	السَّمَآءِ	وَ
Burūj	with (holding)	the Heaven	By

1. By the Heaven, which has *burūj* (castles or watch-towers for security forces),

وَالْيَوْمِ الْمَوْعُوْدِ ﴿٢﴾

الْمَوْعُوْدِ	الْيَوْمِ	وَ
Promised	the Day	By

2. By the Promised Day,

وَشَاهِدٍ وَّمَشْهُوْدٍ ﴿٣﴾

مَشْهُوْدٍ	وَّ	شَاهِدٍ	وَ
Witnessed	And	a witness	By

3. By a witness and a (person or situation) witnessed.

قُتِلَ اَصْحٰبُ الْاُخْدُوْدِ ﴿٤﴾

الْاُخْدُوْدِ	اَصْحٰبُ	قُتِلَ
(of) the Ditches	the People	Ruined are

4. Ruined are the People of the Ditches,

النَّارِ ذَاتِ الْوَقُوْدِ ﴿٥﴾

الْوَقُوْدِ	ذَاتِ	النَّارِ
the fuel	with	The fire

5. (Of) the fire with the fuel.

اِذْ هُمْ عَلَيْهَا قُعُوْدٌ ﴿٦﴾

قُعُوْدٌ	هَا	عَلَيْ	هُمْ	اِذْ
those who sit	its	on side (of it)	they were	Think when

6. Think of the time when they were sitting by the side of the ditches;

وَّهُمْ عَلٰى مَا يَفْعَلُوْنَ بِالْمُؤْمِنِيْنَ شُهُوْدٌ ﴿٧﴾

شُهُوْدٌ	بِالْمُؤْمِنِيْنَ	يَفْعَلُوْنَ	مَا	عَلٰى	هُمْ	وَّ
(were) witnesses	with the believers	they were doing	what	(on)	they (were)	And

7. And they were witnessing what they were doing with the believers.

وَمَا نَقَمُوْا مِنْهُمْ اِلَّآ اَنْ يُّؤْمِنُوْا بِاللّٰهِ الْعَزِيْزِ الْحَمِيْدِ ﴿٨﴾

الْحَمِيْدِ	الْعَزِيْزِ	بِاللّٰهِ	يُّؤْمِنُوْا	اَنْ	اِلَّآ	مِنْهُمْ	نَقَمُوْا	مَا	وَ
Most Praise-worthy	The Almighty	in God	they believed	that	but	(to) them	(they) tortured	not	And

8. And they didn't torture them for any crime but that they believed in (One) God, The Almighty and Most Praiseworthy,

الَّذِيْ لَهٗ مُلْكُ السَّمٰوٰتِ وَالْاَرْضِ ۭ وَاللّٰهُ عَلٰي كُلِّ شَيْءٍ شَهِيْدٌ ۝۹

شَهِيْدٌ	شَيْءٍ	كُلِّ	عَلٰى	وَاللّٰهُ	وَالْاَرْضِ	السَّمٰوٰتِ	مُلْكُ	لَهٗ	الَّذِيْ
(is) a witness	thing	Every	on	and God	and earth	(of) heavens	the kingdom	(owns)	Who

9. To Whom belongs the kingdom of the heavens and the earth, and God is a witness over every thing.

اِنَّ الَّذِيْنَ فَتَنُوا الْمُؤْمِنِيْنَ وَالْمُؤْمِنٰتِ ثُمَّ لَمْ يَتُوْبُوْا

يَتُوْبُوْا	لَمْ	ثُمَّ	الْمُؤْمِنٰتِ	وَ	الْمُؤْمِنِيْنَ	فَتَنُوْا	الَّذِيْنَ	اِنَّ
repented	not	then	believing women	and	believing men	persecut ed	those who	Verily

10. Verily, those who persecuted the believing men and women and then repented not …

فَلَهُمْ عَذَابُ جَهَنَّمَ وَلَهُمْ عَذَابُ الْحَرِيْقِ ۝۱۰

الْحَرِيْقِ	عَذَابُ	لَهُمْ	وَ	جَهَنَّمَ	عَذَابُ	لَهُمْ	فَ
of burning	Punishment	for them	and	of Hell	Punishment	for them	So is

10. ...so for them shall be chastisement of Hell and for them shall be the chastisement of burning.

اِنَّ الَّذِيْنَ اٰمَنُوْا وَعَمِلُوا الصّٰلِحٰتِ لَهُمْ جَنّٰتٌ تَجْرِيْ

تَجْرِيْ	جَنّٰتٌ	لَهُمْ	الصّٰلِحٰتِ	عَمِلُوْا	وَ	اٰمَنُوْا	الَّذِيْنَ	اِنَّ
Flow	Gardens	for them are	virtuous actions	did	and	who believed	those	Verily

11. Verily, those who believed and did virtuous deeds, for them there will be Gardens…

مِنْ تَحْتِهَا الْاَنْهٰرُ ڛ ذٰلِكَ الْفَوْزُ الْكَبِيْرُ ۝۱۱

الْكَبِيْرُ	الْفَوْزُ	ذٰلِكَ	الْاَنْهٰرُ	هَا	تَحْتِ	مِنْ
Supreme	Success	that is	the rivers	which	under	From

11 …under which rivers flow. That is the Supreme Success.

اِنَّ بَطْشَ رَبِّكَ لَشَدِيْدٌ ۝۱۲

شَدِيْدٌ	لَ	رَبِّكَ	بَطْشَ	اِنَّ
(is) terrible	Surely	(of) your Lord	the grip	Indeed

12. Surely, the grip of your Lord is terrible!

إِنَّهٗ هُوَ يُبْدِئُ وَيُعِيْدُ ﴿١٣﴾

يُعِيْدُ	وَ	يُبْدِئُ	هُوَ	إِنَّه
Who will create again	and	Who creates in the first instance	He	Verily (it is He)

13. It is (God) Who creates in the first instance, and it is (God) Who will create again.

وَهُوَ الْغَفُوْرُ الْوَدُوْدُ ﴿١٤﴾

الْوَدُوْد	الْغَفُوْر	هُوَ	وَ
The Most Friendly	The Most Forgiving	He (is)	And

14. And He is (the One) Who is The Most Forgiving, The Most Friendly,

ذُو الْعَرْشِ الْمَجِيْدُ ﴿١٥﴾

الْمَجِيْدُ	الْعَرْشِ	ذُو
The Most Exalted	The Throne	Lord (of)

15. Lord of The Throne, The Most Exalted,

فَعَّالٌ لِّمَا يُرِيْدُ ﴿١٦﴾

يُرِيْدُ	لِّمَا	فَعَّالٌ
He makes up His mind	of what	Doer

16. Doer of what He makes up His mind to do.

هَلْ اَتٰىكَ حَدِيْثُ الْجُنُوْدِ ﴿١٧﴾

الْجُنُوْدِ	حَدِيْثُ	كَ	اَتٰى	هَلْ
the hosts	story of	to you	come	Did

17. Have you received the story of the hosts,

فِرْعَوْنَ وَثَمُوْدَ ﴿١٨﴾

ثَمُوْدَ	وَ	فِرْعَوْنَ
Thamūd	and	Pharaoh

18. (The story of) Pharaoh and Thamūd.

بَلِ الَّذِيْنَ كَفَرُوْا فِيْ تَكْذِيْبٍ ﴿١٩﴾

تَكْذِيْب	فِيْ	كَفَرُوْا	الَّذِيْنَ	بَلِ
giving lie	in (keep)	disbelieved	those who	Nay (And yet)

19. And yet, theose who disbelieved, keep giving lie.

وَّاللّٰهُ مِنْ وَّرَآئِهِمْ مُّحِيْطٌ ﴿٢٠﴾

مُحِيطٌ	هِمْ	وَرَآئِهِ	مِنْ	اللهُ	وَ
encompassing	Them	behind them	from	God (is)	And

20. And God is behind them, encompassing.

بَلْ هُوَ قُرْاٰنٌ مَّجِيدٌ ۝

مَّجِيدٌ	قُرْاٰنٌ	هُوَ	بَلْ
a Majestic	Reader (*Qurʼān*)	it (is)	Nay

21. Nay, it is a Majestic Reader (*Qurʼān*),

فِيْ لَوْحٍ مَّحْفُوْظٍ ۝

مَّحْفُوْظٍ	لَوْحٍ	فِيْ
a Guarded	Tablet	In

22. In a Guarded Tablet.

85 (c) Outline Structure of Sūrah al-Burūj

A. [*Āyāt* 1-4] Introduction of the *sūrah*

The swearing provides a witness for the central theme of the *sūrah*: *It is a serious misunderstanding that a law of the jungle operates in this universe.*

The following story explains the theme: *The losers are the People of the Trenches and not the believers!*

B. [*Āyāt* 5-9] The story is related and reviewed.

The trenches were full of fire. The unjust People of the Trenches, who were burning the believers alive, were adding fuel to it; as they enjoyed watching the scene sitting around these trenches. They were torturing them for the only reason that they believed in The Almighty Praiseworthy God.

C. [*Āyah* 10 & *Āyah* 11] Statement of the Divine Law related with the Ultimate Loss (*Khusrān*) and the Ultimate Success/Happiness (*Falāḥ*) in the Hereafter.

D. [*Āyāt* 12-20] Persecution of the believers will have its cosequences in the Hereafter and also here: history will repeat itself. The believers who are victimized are friends of Almighty God.

**E. [*Āyāt* 21-22] The Qur'anic Movement is well-protected.
It can not be eliminated!**

85 (d) *Sūrah al-Burūj*
Understanding and Interpretation

Sūrah al-Burūj (85) presents the Divine comment on the continuing persecution of the believers by the unjust opponents of the Qur'anic Movements. For this purpose, the *sūrah* reviews an earlier, very severe persecution of believers in One God. The People of the Trenches, who were burning the believers alive, enjoyed seeing this scene, sitting by the side of the trenches. God, Almighty and Praiseworthy, was also watching.

Apparently, God did not take an immediate action. But God shall enter these criminals into the Burning Fire of Hell. God is very forgiving to those who repent and correct themselves. However, God gives severe punishment to those who do not seek God's forgiveness, who do not repent in spite of God's repeated warning. God shall honor the virtuous believers in the Gardens of Paradise.

Even here, in this life, God will take action against the present criminals – the way God punished earlier transgressors, e.g., Thamud and People of Pharaoh. The Divine Forces have already encompassed the enemies. However, the time appointed for the punishment of these criminals has not yet come. Due to this delay, they have developed a misunderstanding that they can do whatever they like and nothing will happen.

(Is the *sūrah* imlicitly suggesting to the wrongdoers: 'why not repent, i.e., make *tawbah* and seek God's forgiveness before the arrival of the Punishment'?)

Chapter Five

86 (a) Sūrah aṭ -Ṭāriq

سُوْرَةُ الطَّارِقِ

بِسْمِ اللّٰهِ الرَّحْمٰنِ الرَّحِيْمِ

وَالسَّمَآءِ وَالطَّارِقِ ۙ﴿١﴾ وَمَآ اَدْرٰىكَ مَا الطَّارِقُ ۙ﴿٢﴾ النَّجْمُ الثَّاقِبُ ۙ﴿٣﴾ اِنْ كُلُّ
نَفْسٍ لَّمَّا عَلَيْهَا حَافِظٌ ؕ﴿٤﴾ فَلْيَنْظُرِ الْاِنْسَانُ مِمَّ خُلِقَ ؕ﴿٥﴾ خُلِقَ مِنْ مَّآءٍ
دَافِقٍ ۙ﴿٦﴾ يَّخْرُجُ مِنْ بَيْنِ الصُّلْبِ وَالتَّرَآئِبِ ؕ﴿٧﴾ اِنَّهٗ عَلٰى رَجْعِهٖ لَقَادِرٌ ؕ﴿٨﴾
يَوْمَ تُبْلَى السَّرَآئِرُ ۙ﴿٩﴾ فَمَا لَهٗ مِنْ قُوَّةٍ وَّلَا نَاصِرٍ ؕ﴿١٠﴾ وَالسَّمَآءِ ذَاتِ الرَّجْعِ ۙ﴿١١﴾
وَالْاَرْضِ ذَاتِ الصَّدْعِ ۙ﴿١٢﴾ اِنَّهٗ لَقَوْلٌ فَصْلٌ ۙ﴿١٣﴾ وَّمَا هُوَ بِالْهَزْلِ ؕ﴿١٤﴾ اِنَّهُمْ
يَكِيْدُوْنَ كَيْدًا ۙ﴿١٥﴾ وَّاَكِيْدُ كَيْدًا ۚ﴿١٦﴾ فَمَهِّلِ الْكٰفِرِيْنَ اَمْهِلْهُمْ رُوَيْدًا ﴿١٧﴾

86 (b) Sūrah aṭ-Ṭāriq

وَالسَّمَآءِ وَالطَّارِقِ ۝١

الطَّارِقِ	وَ	السَّمَآءِ	وَ
the Night Visitant	and	the Heaven	By

1. By the Heaven and the Night Visitant.

وَمَآ أَدْرٰىكَ مَا الطَّارِقُ ۝٢

الطَّارِقُ	مَا	كَ	أَدْرٰى	مَآ	وَ
the Night Visitant	what is	you	make understand	what	And

2. And what will make you understand what the Night Visitant is?

النَّجْمُ الثَّاقِبُ ۝٣

الثَّاقِبُ	النَّجْمُ
(of) piercing brightness	The star

3. The star of piercing brightness.

إِنْ كُلُّ نَفْسٍ لَّمَّا عَلَيْهَا حَافِظٌ ۝٤

حَافِظٌ	عَلَيْهَا	لَّمَّا	نَفْسٍ	كُلُّ	إِنْ
a guard	on him	that there remains	person	each	It is true of

4. (It is true of) each person (that) a guard (angel) is, all the time, (watching) over him/her.

فَلْيَنْظُرِ الْإِنْسَانُ مِمَّ خُلِقَ ۝٥

خُلِقَ	مِمَّ	الْإِنْسَانُ	يَنْظُرِ	لْ	فَ
he is created	from what	the human	see	let	So

5. So, let human see from what he/she is created.

خُلِقَ مِنْ مَّآءٍ دَافِقٍ ۝٦

دَافِقٍ	مَّآءٍ	مِنْ	خُلِقَ
which ejectes	water	from	He is created

6. He/she is created from a water (drop) that gushes out.

يَخْرُجُ مِنۢ بَيْنِ الصُّلْبِ وَالتَّرَآئِبِ ۝٧

التَّرَائِبِ	وَ	الصُّلْبِ	بَيْنِ	مِن	يَخْرُجُ
the ribs	and	the backbone	between	from	It comes out

7. (It) comes out from (somewhere) between the backbone and the ribs.

إِنَّهُۥ عَلَىٰ رَجْعِهِۦ لَقَادِرٌ ۝٨

قَادِرٌ	لَ	رَجْعِه	عَلٰى	اِنَّه
Powerful	surely	making him return	on	Verily, God is

8. God (who created first time) has power to bring him/her back (to life again after his/her death).

يَوْمَ تُبْلَى السَّرَآئِرُ ۝٩

السَّرَائِرُ	تُبْلَى	يَوْمَ
the secrets	will be tried	That day

9. (Think of) that day, when secrets will be tried.

فَمَا لَهُۥ مِن قُوَّةٍ وَلَا نَاصِرٍ ۝١٠

نَاصِرٍ	لَا	وَ	قُوَّةٍ	مِنْ	لَه	مَا	فَ
Helper	no	and	strength	any	for him	(is) not	So

10. So, he (criminal) will have no strength and no helper for (to defend) oneself.

وَالسَّمَآءِ ذَاتِ الرَّجْعِ ۝١١

الرَّجْعِ	ذَاتِ	السَّمَاءِ	وَ
returns	(which has) with	the Heaven	By

11. By the Heaven which returns (in its rotations to the same position.).

وَالْأَرْضِ ذَاتِ الصَّدْعِ ۝١٢

الصَّدْعِ	ذَاتِ	الْأَرْضِ	وَ
splits	(which)	the Earth	By

12. By the Earth which splits (for the sprouting of vegetation).

إِنَّهُۥ لَقَوْلٌ فَصْلٌ ۝١٣

فَصْلٌ	قَوْلٌ	لَ	اِنَّه
decisive	a word	surely	Verily, it (the Qur'an) is

13. Surely, it (the Qur'an) is a Decisive Word.

وَّمَا هُوَ بِالْهَزْلِ ﴿١٤﴾

بِالْهَزْلِ	هُوَ	مَا	وَّ
(for amusment) a joke	it	(is) not	And

14. And it is no joke.

اِنَّهُمْ يَكِيْدُوْنَ كَيْدًا ﴿١٥﴾

كَيْدًا	يَكِيْدُوْنَ	هُمْ	اِنَّ
a plot	(are) plotting	they	Verily,

15. Verily, they are hatching a plot.

وَّاَكِيْدُ كَيْدًا ﴿١٦﴾

كَيْدًا	اَكِيْدُ	وَّ
a plot	I am plotting	And

16. And I am (also) hatching a plot.

فَمَهِّلِ الْكٰفِرِيْنَ اَمْهِلْهُمْ رُوَيْدًا ﴿١٧﴾

رُوَيْدًا	اَمْهِلْهُمْ	الْكٰفِرِيْنَ	فَمَهِّلِ
a little	give respite to them	to the disblievers	So give respite

17. So, respite the disbelievers, put up with them for a while.

86 (c) Outline Structure of Sūrah aṭ-Ṭāriq

There are objects which exist but we do not see them:

A. **[*Āyāt* 1-3] See the example of a shining Evening Star, which remained unseen throughout the day.**

B. **[*Āyah* 4]: Likewise, we do not see but an angel-guard is appointed on each of us: it will be visible to us only on the Judgement Day.**

C. **[*Āyāt* 5-7] Consider: 'an individual's stepping into this world.'**
Do we know from where our creation is originated?
All we see is a drop being ejected from within a human body!
(This very soon becomes a human embryo!)

D. [**Āyāt** 8-10] But '**Where do we go when we leave this world?**'
We go back to God from Whom our creation proceeded earlier.
God has power to give us life again after our death.
That day many crimes, hidden from our eyes will be tried.
Those found guilty will not be able to defend themselves.
Nor others will be able to help them.

E. **[*Āyah* 11 & *Āyah* 12] Present two witnesses:**
'the Heaven that returns'
and 'the Earth that splits.'
Today, after each rotation the Heaven returns to a similar position.
That day, its rotations will bring into existence a whole new world.
Today the earth splits with a verdure.
That day, dead bodies will be coming out of it alive.

F. **[*Āyāt* 13-17] conclude: it is a decisive word; it is not a joke.**
O Prophet! They are plotting against you.
But God is also plotting against them.
(The Divine Punishment is on its way.)

Just give them a little respite!

86 (d) Sūrah aṭ-Ṭāriq
Understanding and Interpretation

Sūrah aṭ-Ṭāriq (86) argues: If you do not see the Divine forces (85: 20) which are ready to punish the criminals, it does not mean that they do not exist!

It raises the Question: Did the bright evening star cease to exist during the day?

Likewise, the *sūrah* informs: only on Judgment Day, the sceptics will realize that throughout this worldly life 'a guardian-angel' remained with them.

Do we know where was our existence before we entered into this world? We can go only up to a certain point. A drop of a fluid-like object gushed forth from somewhere and later it developed into a human embryo.

Likewise, we do not see where people go after their death. Those who do not believe in life after death will actually see on the Day of Judgment that God, Who created us the first time, will again bring us back to life a second time. That day many secret crimes will be made known and given an open trial. The criminals who committed those crimes, unknown to others, will be punished and no one will be able to help them.

At this point, the *sūrah* brings one swearing in *āyah* 86:11 and another in *āyah* 86:12. The *āyah* (86:11) suggests that the heavenly rotations will continue on the same pattern for some time; but then *a whole new world* will be brought into existence on the Judgment Day. The *āyah* 86:12 suggests this will be the day when the earth will crack open with dead bodies coming out of it alive - the way today it splits with the growth of plants and trees.

In light of the above, the *sūrah* concludes: Do not take the Divine Book lightly. What it says is a serious matter. It informs: The enemies are plotting against the Qur'anic Movement. They do not see, God's hidden plot is ready to punish them.

Chapter Six

87 (a) Sūrah al-A'lā

سَبِّحِ اسْمَ رَبِّكَ الْاَعْلَى ۙ﴿۱﴾ الَّذِيْ خَلَقَ فَسَوّٰى ۙ﴿۲﴾ وَالَّذِيْ قَدَّرَ فَهَدٰى ۙ﴿۳﴾ وَ

الَّذِيْٓ اَخْرَجَ الْمَرْعٰى ۙ﴿۴﴾ فَجَعَلَهٗ غُثَآءً اَحْوٰى ؕ﴿۵﴾ سَنُقْرِئُكَ فَلَا تَنْسٰٓى ۙ﴿۶﴾ اِلَّا

مَا شَآءَ اللّٰهُ ؕ اِنَّهٗ يَعْلَمُ الْجَهْرَ وَمَا يَخْفٰى ؕ﴿۷﴾ وَنُيَسِّرُكَ لِلْيُسْرٰى ۚ﴿۸﴾ فَذَكِّرْ

اِنْ نَّفَعَتِ الذِّكْرٰى ؕ﴿۹﴾ سَيَذَّكَّرُ مَنْ يَّخْشٰى ۙ﴿۱۰﴾ وَيَتَجَنَّبُهَا الْاَشْقَى ۙ﴿۱۱﴾ الَّذِيْ

يَصْلَى النَّارَ الْكُبْرٰى ۚ﴿۱۲﴾ ثُمَّ لَا يَمُوْتُ فِيْهَا وَلَا يَحْيٰى ؕ﴿۱۳﴾ قَدْ اَفْلَحَ مَنْ

تَزَكّٰى ۙ﴿۱۴﴾ وَذَكَرَ اسْمَ رَبِّهٖ فَصَلّٰى ؕ﴿۱۵﴾ بَلْ تُؤْثِرُوْنَ الْحَيٰوةَ الدُّنْيَا ۫ۖ﴿۱۶﴾ وَالْاٰخِرَةُ

خَيْرٌ وَّاَبْقٰى ؕ﴿۱۷﴾ اِنَّ هٰذَا لَفِي الصُّحُفِ الْاُوْلٰى ۙ﴿۱۸﴾ صُحُفِ اِبْرٰهِيْمَ وَمُوْسٰى ﴿۱۹﴾

87 (b) Sūrah al-A'lā

سَبِّحِ اسْمَ رَبِّكَ الْاَعْلَى ١			
الْاَعْلَى	رَبِّكَ	اسْمَ	سَبِّحِ
The Most High	(of) your Lord	the name	Glorify
1. Glorify the name of your Lord, The Most High.			

الَّذِيْ خَلَقَ فَسَوّٰى ٢		
فَسَوّٰى	خَلَقَ	الَّذِيْ
so He perfected	created	Who
2. Who created then He perfected (i.e., gave finishing touches).		

وَالَّذِيْ قَدَّرَ فَهَدٰى ٣			
فَهَدٰى	قَدَّرَ	الَّذِيْ	وَ
and then guided	Planned	Who	And
3. And Who planned and then guided.			

وَالَّذِيْٓ اَخْرَجَ الْمَرْعٰى ٤			
الْمَرْعٰى	اَخْرَجَ	الَّذِيْٓ	وَ
the pasturage	brought out	Who	And
4. And Who brought out the pasturage.			

فَجَعَلَهٗ غُثَآءً اَحْوٰى ٥				
اَحْوٰى	غُثَآءً	هٗ	جَعَلَ	فَ
black	a rubbish	it	God made	So
5. So (through a step by step process), (God) turned it into a black rubbish.				

سَنُقْرِئُكَ فَلَا تَنْسٰٓى ٦					
تَنْسٰٓى	لَا	فَ	كَ	نُقْرِئُ	سَ
you will forgot	not	So	you	We shall teach	Soon
6. Soon We shall teach you, so you will not forget.					

اِلَّا مَا شَآءَ اللّٰهُ اِنَّهٗ يَعْلَمُ الْجَهْرَ وَمَا يَخْفٰى ٧								
يَخْفٰى	وَمَا	الْجَهْرَ	يَعْلَمُ	اِنَّهٗ	اللّٰهُ	شَآءَ	مَا	اِلَّا
is hidden	and that which	the open	God knows	verily	Allah	wills	what	But
7. But what God wills. Verily, God knows what is open and what is hidden.								

وَنُيَسِّرُكَ لِلْيُسْرٰى ۝٨

يُسْرٰى	لْ	لِ	كَ	نُيَسِّرُ	وَ
Easy (Path)	the	for	you	We shall prepare	And

8. And We shall prepare you for the Easy Path.

فَذَكِّرْ اِنْ نَّفَعَتِ الذِّكْرٰى ۝٩

الذِّكْرٰى	نَّفَعَتِ	اِنْ	ذَكِّرْ	فَ
the reminding	benefits	if	remind	So

9. So remind, if the reminding benefits.

سَيَذَّكَّرُ مَنْ يَّخْشٰى ۝١٠

يَّخْشٰى	مَنْ	يَذَّكَّرُ	سَ
fears	(one) who	will be reminded	Soon

10. Soon one who fears will be reminded (and receive the benefit).

وَيَتَجَنَّبُهَا الْاَشْقَى ۝١١

الْاَشْقَى	هَا	يَتَجَنَّبُ	وَ
the most wretched	(from) it	will turn aside	And

11. And the most wretched will turn aside from it.

الَّذِيْ يَصْلَى النَّارَ الْكُبْرٰى ۝١٢

الْكُبْرٰى	النَّارَ	يَصْلَى	الَّذِيْ
the great	(in) the fire	will roast	Who

12. Who will roast in the Great Fire.

ثُمَّ لَا يَمُوْتُ فِيْهَا وَلَا يَحْيٰى ۝١٣

يَحْيٰى	وَلَا	هَا	فِيْ	يَمُوْتُ	لَا	ثُمَّ
live	nor	it	In	will (he) die	neither	Then

13. Then he will neither die in it, nor live!

قَدْ اَفْلَحَ مَنْ تَزَكّٰى ۝١٤

تَزَكّٰى	مَنْ	اَفْلَحَ	قَدْ
(took care) of his *tazkiyah*	who	he has succeeded	Indeed

14. He/she has achieved *Falāḥ* (Ultimate Happiness/Success) who takes care of one's own spiritual and moral development.

وَذَكَرَ اسْمَ رَبِّهٖ فَصَلّٰى ۝١٥

صَلّٰى	فَ	رَبِّهٖ	اسْمَ	ذَكَرَ	وَ
offered *ṣalāh*	and	(of) his Lord	the name	he remembered	And

15. And he remembered the name of his/her Lord and offered prayer (made *ṣalāh*).

بَلْ تُؤْثِرُوْنَ الْحَيٰوةَ الدُّنْيَا ﴿١٦﴾

الدُّنْيَا	الْحَيٰوةَ	تُؤْثِرُوْنَ	بَلْ
this wordly	life	you prefer	Nay

16. Instead you prefer this worldly life.

وَالْاٰخِرَةُ خَيْرٌ وَّاَبْقٰى ﴿١٧﴾

اَبْقٰى	وَّ	خَيْرٌ	الْاٰخِرَةُ	وَ
more lasting	and	(is) better	the Hereafter	And

17. Whereas the Hereafter is better and everlasting.

اِنَّ هٰذَا لَفِي الصُّحُفِ الْاُوْلٰى ﴿١٨﴾

الْاُوْلٰى	الصُّحُفِ	فِي	لَ	هٰذَا	اِنَّ
the earlier	scriptures	in	surely	this (is)	Verily

18. Verily, this is (written) in the earlier scriptures.

صُحُفِ اِبْرٰهِيْمَ وَمُوْسٰى ﴿١٩﴾

مُوْسٰى	وَ	اِبْرٰهِيْمَ	صُحُفِ
Moses	and	(of) Abraham	Scriptures

19. The scriptures of Abraham and Moses.

87 (c) Outline Structure of Sūrah al-A'lā

This *sūrah* makes its point in five stages:

A. **[*Āyah* 1] '*Tazkiyah* through *dhikr*' is the central theme:** Qur'anic Movement is an invitation to make *tasbīḥ* (to say '*subḥānallāh*' 'glory be to God' with the whole of one's being).The Prophet is commanded to (make *sajdah, i.e.,* to prostrate) saying, 'I glorify My Lord, The Most High!'

B. **[*Āyāt* 2-5] The whole world of *khalq* (creation*)* and '*amr* (governance) is glorifying God:** Whatever God creates, God creates perfectly. God has a plan for each object's life's journey and guides it accordingly. Example: stage by stage growth and decay of the pasturage.

C. **[*Āyāt* 6-13] God guides the Prophet to lead future spiritual and moral progress of humankind:**

7: 6-7: God will teach you what you shall not forget….
7: 8: And prepare you for the Easy Journey to God
7: 9-13: Watch how your reminding is working; give more attention to those concerned (with their *tazkiyah*).
………………

D. **[*Āyāt* 14-15] Summarize the central theme of the *sūrah*.**

Those who take care of their *tazkiyah;*
remember God, offer *ṣalāh*......
already achieved *Falāḥ* (Ultimate Success/Happiness)!

E. **[*Āyāt* 16-19] What is important:** as earlier scriptures underlined, most people are so involved in this worldly life, that they neglect *Ākhirah* and do not take care of their *tazkiyah.*

87 (d) Sūrah al-A'lā
Understanding and Interpretation

The sūrah elaborates the point of glorification and defines its relationship with tazkiyah, which is the key to Falāḥ.

God's creation is perfect. And Divine Guidance for each creature is well-planned. Just consider the growth and decay of the pasture. Likewise, the whole universe is glorifying God.

God created humans with immense possibilities of spiritual and moral progress and guides them through a step-by-step process. At this stage of the history of the prophetic movement, God will be teaching the Book to the Prophet, in the most perfect manner. *Through teaching him the Book, God is preparing the Prophet to do his job which includes tadhkīr as well as tazkiyah.*

When the Prophet invites the people to the remembrance of God, he should watch how his *tadhkır* (reminding) is working. Then he should pay more heed – by way of *tazkiyah* - to those who are concerned with their own spiritual and moral development.

Those, who turn away from the reminding, will be deprived of guidance and thereby *tazkiyah.* They will be punished in the Hell Fire.

The deciding factor here is: 'does one really care for the Hereafter?' Those who are lost in immediate pleasures of this life will fail to receive any benefit from Divine Guidance – no *tadhkīr* will work with them, no *tazkiyah* will initiate. This was the teaching of earlier scriptures, e.g., of Abraham and Moses.

Chapter Seven

88 (a) Sūrah al-Ghāshiyah

سُوْرَةُ الْغَاشِيَةِ

بِسْمِ اللّٰهِ الرَّحْمٰنِ الرَّحِيْمِ

هَلْ اَتٰىكَ حَدِيْثُ الْغَاشِيَةِ ﴿١﴾ وُجُوْهٌ يَّوْمَئِذٍ خَاشِعَةٌ ﴿٢﴾ عَامِلَةٌ نَّاصِبَةٌ ﴿٣﴾

تَصْلٰى نَارًا حَامِيَةً ﴿٤﴾ تُسْقٰى مِنْ عَيْنٍ اٰنِيَةٍ ﴿٥﴾ لَيْسَ لَهُمْ طَعَامٌ اِلَّا مِنْ

ضَرِيْعٍ ﴿٦﴾ لَّا يُسْمِنُ وَلَا يُغْنِيْ مِنْ جُوْعٍ ﴿٧﴾ وُجُوْهٌ يَّوْمَئِذٍ نَّاعِمَةٌ ﴿٨﴾ لِّسَعْيِهَا

رَاضِيَةٌ ﴿٩﴾ فِيْ جَنَّةٍ عَالِيَةٍ ﴿١٠﴾ لَّا تَسْمَعُ فِيْهَا لَاغِيَةً ﴿١١﴾ فِيْهَا عَيْنٌ جَارِيَةٌ ﴿١٢﴾

فِيْهَا سُرُرٌ مَّرْفُوْعَةٌ ﴿١٣﴾ وَّاَكْوَابٌ مَّوْضُوْعَةٌ ﴿١٤﴾ وَّنَمَارِقُ مَصْفُوْفَةٌ ﴿١٥﴾ وَّزَرَابِيُّ

مَبْثُوْثَةٌ ﴿١٦﴾ اَفَلَا يَنْظُرُوْنَ اِلَى الْاِبِلِ كَيْفَ خُلِقَتْ ﴿١٧﴾ وَاِلَى السَّمَآءِ كَيْفَ

رُفِعَتْ ﴿١٨﴾ وَاِلَى الْجِبَالِ كَيْفَ نُصِبَتْ ﴿١٩﴾ وَاِلَى الْاَرْضِ كَيْفَ سُطِحَتْ ﴿٢٠﴾

فَذَكِّرْ اِنَّمَآ اَنْتَ مُذَكِّرٌ ﴿٢١﴾ لَسْتَ عَلَيْهِمْ بِمُصَيْطِرٍ ﴿٢٢﴾ اِلَّا مَنْ تَوَلّٰى وَكَفَرَ ﴿٢٣﴾

فَيُعَذِّبُهُ اللّٰهُ الْعَذَابَ الْاَكْبَرَ ﴿٢٤﴾ اِنَّ اِلَيْنَآ اِيَابَهُمْ ﴿٢٥﴾ ثُمَّ اِنَّ عَلَيْنَا

حِسَابَهُمْ ﴿٢٦﴾

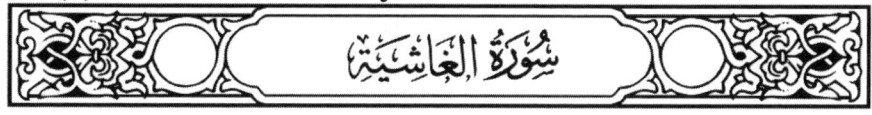

88 (b) Sūrah al-Ghāshiyah

هَلْ اَتٰىكَ حَدِيْثُ الْغَاشِيَةِ ؕ ﴿١﴾

الْغَاشِيَةِ	حَدِيْثُ	كَ	اَتٰى	هَلْ
(of) The All- Pervading Event	the account	(to) you	come	Did ?

1. Has there come to you the account of The All-Pervading Event?

وُجُوْهٌ يَّوْمَئِذٍ خَاشِعَةٌ ۙ ﴿٢﴾

خَاشِعَةٌ	يَّوْمَئِذٍ	وُجُوْهٌ
will be downcast	(on) that day	(So many) faces

2. Many human beings (faces) on that day will be downcast.

عَامِلَةٌ نَّاصِبَةٌ ۙ ﴿٣﴾ تَصْلٰى نَارًا حَامِيَةً ۙ ﴿٤﴾

حَامِيَةً	نَارًا	تَصْلٰى	نَّاصِبَةٌ	عَامِلَةٌ
scorching	(in) a fire	(will) roast	toil-worn	Laboring

4. (Will) roast in a scorching Fire 3. Laboring, toil-worn!

تُسْقٰى مِنْ عَيْنٍ اٰنِيَةٍ ؕ ﴿٥﴾

اٰنِيَةٍ	عَيْنٍ	مِنْ	تُسْقٰى
(of) boiling water	a spring	from	Made to drink

5. Made to drink from a spring of boiling water.

لَيْسَ لَهُمْ طَعَامٌ اِلَّا مِنْ ضَرِيْعٍ ۙ ﴿٦﴾

ضَرِيْعٍ	مِنْ	اِلَّا	طَعَامٌ	لَهُمْ	لَيْسَ
cactus	Some	except	food	for them	There (will be) no

6. There will be no food for them except some cactus.

لَّا يُسْمِنُ وَلَا يُغْنِيْ مِنْ جُوْعٍ ؕ ﴿٧﴾

جُوْعٍ	مِنْ	يُغْنِيْ	لَا	وَ	يُسْمِنُ	لَّا
hunger	(from)	does satisfy	not	and	(having) a nutritious value	Not

7. Having no nutritious value, and does not satisfy hunger.

وُجُوْهٌ يَّوْمَئِذٍ نَّاعِمَةٌ ۙ ﴿٨﴾

نَّاعِمَةٌ	يَّوْمَئِذٍ	وُجُوْهٌ
(will be) blissful	on that day	(So many) faces

8. Many human beings (faces) will be blissful on that Day.

لِّسَعْيِهَا رَاضِيَةٌ ۙ ﴿٩﴾ فِيْ جَنَّةٍ عَالِيَةٍ ۙ ﴿١٠﴾

عَالِيَةٍ	جَنَّةٍ	فِيْ	رَاضِيَةٌ	سَعْيِهَا	لِّ
lofty	a garden	In	pleased	their efforts	For

10. (Dwelling) in a lofty garden. 9. Pleased with their efforts.

لَّا تَسْمَعُ فِيْهَا لَاغِيَةً ١١

لَاغِيَةً	هَا	فِيْ	تَسْمَعُ	لَّا
loose talk	It	in	you hear	Do not

11. You do not hear any loose talk in it.

فِيْهَا عَيْنٌ جَارِيَةٌ ١٢ فِيْهَا سُرُرٌ مَّرْفُوْعَةٌ ١٣

مَّرْفُوْعَةٌ	سُرُرٌ	فِيْهَا	جَارِيَةٌ	عَيْنٌ	فِيْهَا
raised up	couches	In it	flowing	(there is) a spring	In it

13. Therein are couches raised up. 12. Therein is a flowing spring.

وَّ اَكْوَابٌ مَّوْضُوْعَةٌ ١٤ وَّ نَمَارِقُ مَصْفُوْفَةٌ ١٥

مَصْفُوْفَةٌ	نَمَارِقُ	وَّ	مَّوْضُوْعَةٌ	اَكْوَابٌ	وَّ
arranged	cushions	And	set forth	goblets	And

15. And cushions arranged, 14. And goblets set forth,

وَّ زَرَابِيُّ مَبْثُوْثَةٌ ١٦

مَبْثُوْثَةٌ	زَرَابِيُّ	وَّ
Outspread	carpets	And

16. And carpets outspread.

اَفَلَا يَنْظُرُوْنَ اِلَى الْاِبِلِ كَيْفَ خُلِقَتْ ١٧

خُلِقَتْ	كَيْفَ	الْاِبِلِ	اِلَى	يَنْظُرُوْنَ	اَفَلَا
is it created	How	the camel	at	look	Do (they) not

17. Do they not see the camel, the way it is created!

وَاِلَى السَّمَآءِ كَيْفَ رُفِعَتْ ١٨

رُفِعَتْ	كَيْفَ	السَّمَآءِ	اِلَى	وَ
it is raised so high	How	the heaven	at	And

18. And at the heaven, the way it is raised (so) high!

وَاِلَى الْجِبَالِ كَيْفَ نُصِبَتْ ١٩

نُصِبَتْ	كَيْفَ	الْجِبَالِ	اِلَى	وَ
they are fixed	How	the mountains	at	And

19. And at the mountains, the way they are fixed (so firmly)!

وَإِلَى الْأَرْضِ كَيْفَ سُطِحَتْ ﴿٢٠﴾

سُطِحَتْ	كَيْفَ	الْأَرْضِ	إِلَى	وَ
it is spread	how	the Earth	at	And

20. And at the Earth, the way it is spread (and made livable for humans)!

فَذَكِّرْ إِنَّمَا أَنْتَ مُذَكِّرٌ ﴿٢١﴾

مُذَكِّرٌ	أَنْتَ	إِنَّمَا	ذَكِّرْ	فَ
(are) a reminder	You	verily	remind them	So

21. So, give them the reminding, you are only the one (whose duty) is to remind.

لَسْتَ عَلَيْهِمْ بِمُصَيْطِرٍ ﴿٢٢﴾

مُصَيْطِرٍ	بِ	هِمْ	عَلَيْ	لَسْتَ
a controller	.....	them	upon	You are not

22. You are not charged to compel them.

إِلَّا مَنْ تَوَلَّىٰ وَكَفَرَ ﴿٢٣﴾

كَفَرَ	وَ	تَوَلَّىٰ	مَنْ	إِلَّا
disbelieved	And	turned away	one who	But

23. But one who turned away and disbelieved (rejects your call),

فَيُعَذِّبُهُ اللَّهُ الْعَذَابَ الْأَكْبَرَ ﴿٢٤﴾

الْأَكْبَرَ	الْعَذَابَ	اللَّهُ	هُ	يُعَذِّبُ	فَ
most severe (greatest)	the punishment	God	him	will punish	So

24. So God will punish him with the most severe punishment.

إِنَّ إِلَيْنَا إِيَابَهُمْ ﴿٢٥﴾

هُمْ	إِيَابَ	نَا	إِلَيْ	إِنَّ
their	(is) return	Us	to	Verily

25. Verily, to Us is their return.

ثُمَّ إِنَّ عَلَيْنَا حِسَابَهُمْ ﴿٢٦﴾

هُمْ	حِسَابَ	نَا	عَلَيْ	إِنَّ	ثُمَّ
(is) their	checking of account	Us	upon	verily	Then

26. Then,verily, it is upon Us to call them to account.

88 (c) Outline Structureof Sūrah al-Ghāshiyah

This *sūrah* makes its point in four stages:

A. **[*Āyāt* 1-16] present *ākhirah* in three steps**.

Āyah **1:** it is an all-Pervading Reality.

A*yāt* **2-7** deal with the fate of the wretched.

Āyāt **8-16** deal with the fate of the virtuous.

B. [*Āyāt* 17-20] invite us to reflection:
What kind of home has God furnished for us in this life?

C. [*Āyāt* 21-24] Prophet's job is reminding (*tadhkīr*) only.

It is not his responsibility to make people follow guidance.
God will take care of the criminals.

D. **[*Āyah* 25 and 26] together make the concluding remark:**

Ultimately the people will come back to God.
And then God will call them to account.

88 (d) Sūrah al-Ghāshiyah
Understanding and Interpretation

Sūrah al-Ghāshiyah (88) discusses in detail the two faces of the 'all-Pervading Reality of *Ākhirah'* – the fate of the wretched as well as that of the God-fearing.

The question arises 'why are the people so unconcerned with their own destiny?' The *Sūrah al-Ghāshiyah* (88), implicitly suggests: it is lack of thinking that is the cause of their negligence and ingratitude. The *sūrah,* therefore, calls the people to open their eyes and see what a wonderful world God had created for them! Then what is the justification for their ingratitude?

However, if the people do not reflect and they conduct their lives thanklessly, the prophet should not be so concerned. The Prophet's responsibility is just to remind them. It is not his duty to force them to the right path.

At the end they will return to their Lord and they themselves will have to account for what they did.

Chapter Eight

89 (a) Sūrah al-Fajr

سُوْرَةُ الْفَجْرِ

بِسْمِ اللّٰهِ الرَّحْمٰنِ الرَّحِيْمِ

وَالْفَجْرِ ﴿١﴾ وَلَيَالٍ عَشْرٍ ﴿٢﴾ وَّالشَّفْعِ وَالْوَتْرِ ﴿٣﴾ وَالَّيْلِ اِذَا يَسْرِ ﴿٤﴾ هَلْ فِيْ
ذٰلِكَ قَسَمٌ لِّذِيْ حِجْرٍ ﴿٥﴾ اَلَمْ تَرَ كَيْفَ فَعَلَ رَبُّكَ بِعَادٍ ﴿٦﴾ اِرَمَ ذَاتِ
الْعِمَادِ ﴿٧﴾ الَّتِيْ لَمْ يُخْلَقْ مِثْلُهَا فِي الْبِلَادِ ﴿٨﴾ وَثَمُوْدَ الَّذِيْنَ جَابُوا الصَّخْرَ
بِالْوَادِ ﴿٩﴾ وَفِرْعَوْنَ ذِي الْاَوْتَادِ ﴿١٠﴾ الَّذِيْنَ طَغَوْا فِي الْبِلَادِ ﴿١١﴾ فَاَكْثَرُوْا فِيْهَا
الْفَسَادَ ﴿١٢﴾ فَصَبَّ عَلَيْهِمْ رَبُّكَ سَوْطَ عَذَابٍ ﴿١٣﴾ اِنَّ رَبَّكَ لَبِالْمِرْصَادِ ﴿١٤﴾ فَاَمَّا
الْاِنْسَانُ اِذَا مَا ابْتَلٰىهُ رَبُّهٗ فَاَكْرَمَهٗ وَنَعَّمَهٗ فَيَقُوْلُ رَبِّيْٓ اَكْرَمَنِ ﴿١٥﴾ وَاَمَّآ
اِذَا مَا ابْتَلٰىهُ فَقَدَرَ عَلَيْهِ رِزْقَهٗ فَيَقُوْلُ رَبِّيْٓ اَهَانَنِ ﴿١٦﴾ كَلَّا بَلْ لَّا تُكْرِمُوْنَ
الْيَتِيْمَ ﴿١٧﴾ وَلَا تَحٰٓضُّوْنَ عَلٰى طَعَامِ الْمِسْكِيْنِ ﴿١٨﴾ وَتَاْكُلُوْنَ التُّرَاثَ اَكْلًا
لَّمًّا ﴿١٩﴾ وَّتُحِبُّوْنَ الْمَالَ حُبًّا جَمًّا ﴿٢٠﴾ كَلَّآ اِذَا دُكَّتِ الْاَرْضُ دَكًّا دَكًّا ﴿٢١﴾ وَّجَآءَ
رَبُّكَ وَالْمَلَكُ صَفًّا صَفًّا ﴿٢٢﴾ وَجِايْٓءَ يَوْمَئِذٍ بِجَهَنَّمَ يَوْمَئِذٍ يَّتَذَكَّرُ
الْاِنْسَانُ وَاَنّٰى لَهُ الذِّكْرٰى ﴿٢٣﴾ يَقُوْلُ يٰلَيْتَنِيْ قَدَّمْتُ لِحَيَاتِيْ ﴿٢٤﴾ فَيَوْمَئِذٍ لَّا
يُعَذِّبُ عَذَابَهٗٓ اَحَدٌ ﴿٢٥﴾ وَّلَا يُوْثِقُ وَثَاقَهٗٓ اَحَدٌ ﴿٢٦﴾ يٰٓاَيَّتُهَا النَّفْسُ الْمُطْمَئِنَّةُ ﴿٢٧﴾
ارْجِعِيْٓ اِلٰى رَبِّكِ رَاضِيَةً مَّرْضِيَّةً ﴿٢٨﴾ فَادْخُلِيْ فِيْ عِبٰدِيْ ﴿٢٩﴾ وَادْخُلِيْ جَنَّتِيْ ﴿٣٠﴾

89 (b) Word by word translation of Sūrah al-Fajr

وَالْفَجْرِ ۝١ وَلَيَالٍ عَشْرٍ ۝٢

عَشْرٍ	لَيَالٍ	وَ	الْفَجْرِ	وَ
Ten	nights	By	the dawn	By

1. By the dawn, 2. By ten nights,

وَّالشَّفْعِ وَالْوَتْرِ ۝٣

الْوَتْرِ	وَ	الشَّفْعِ	وَّ
the odd	And	the even	By

3. By The Even and The Odd,

وَالَّيْلِ اِذَا يَسْرِ ۝٤

يَسْرِ	اِذَا	الَّيْلِ	وَ
(it) departs	When	the night	By

4. By the night when it departs.

هَلْ فِيْ ذٰلِكَ قَسَمٌ لِّذِيْ حِجْرٍ ۝٥

ذِيْ حِجْرٍ	لِّ	قَسَمٌ	ذٰلِكَ	فِيْ	هَلْ
one who has understanding	for	a swearing	that	in	Is (there)

5. Is there in that, a swearing, for one who has understanding?

اَلَمْ تَرَ كَيْفَ فَعَلَ رَبُّكَ بِعَادٍ ۝٦

عَادٍ	بِ	كَ	رَبُّ	فَعَلَ	كَيْفَ	تَرَ	اَلَمْ
‘Ād	with	Your	Lord	deal	how	you see	Did (you) not

6. Did you not see how your Lord dealt with ‘Ād?

اِرَمَ ذَاتِ الْعِمَادِ ۝٧

الْعِمَادِ	ذَاتِ	اِرَمَ
pillars	With	Iram

7. (That is,) Iram, the People of (tall) Pillars,

الَّتِيْ لَمْ يُخْلَقْ مِثْلُهَا فِي الْبِلَادِ ۝٨

الْبِلَادِ	فِي	هَا	مِثْلُ	يُخْلَقْ	لَمْ	الَّتِيْ
the cities	In	Them	like	was created	not	Those

8. The like of which was not created in the cities,

وَثَمُوْدَ الَّذِيْنَ جَابُوا الصَّخْرَ بِالْوَادِ ۙ﴿٩﴾

الْوَادِ	بِ	الصَّخْرَ	جَابُو	الَّذِيْنَ	ثَمُوْدَ	وَ
the valley	in	rocks	carved	who	Thamūd	And

9. And the Thamūd who carved rocks out of the valley,

وَفِرْعَوْنَ ذِي الْاَوْتَادِ ۙ﴿١٠﴾

الْاَوْتَادِ	ذِي	فِرْعَوْنَ	وَ
(The Lord) of Stakes	(with)	Pharaoh	And

10. And Pharaoh, Lord of Stakes.

الَّذِيْنَ طَغَوْا فِي الْبِلَادِ ۙ﴿١١﴾

الْبِلَادِ	فِي	طَغَوْا	الَّذِيْنَ
the cities	in	transgressed	Who

11. These were the people who (all) transgressed in the cities.

فَاَكْثَرُوْا فِيْهَا الْفَسَادَ ۙ﴿١٢﴾

الْفَسَادَ	هَا	فِيْ	اَكْثَرُوْا	فَ
corruption	it (their cities)	in	Added	Thereby

12. And increased corruption (in their cities)

فَصَبَّ عَلَيْهِمْ رَبُّكَ سَوْطَ عَذَابٍ ۚ﴿١٣﴾

عَذَابٍ	سَوْطَ	كَ	رَبُّ	هِمْ	عَلَيْ	صَبَّ	فَ
torment (of)	Scourage	your	Lord	them	upon	unleashed	Therefore

13. Therefore, your Lord unleashed the scourge of torment upon them.

اِنَّ رَبَّكَ لَبِالْمِرْصَادِ ۭ﴿١٤﴾

الْمِرْصَادِ	بِ	لَ	كَ	رَبَّ	اِنَّ
Watch	(with)	(is) surely	Your	Lord	Verily

14. Verily, your Lord is on the watch (today also)!

فَاَمَّا الْاِنْسَانُ اِذَا مَا ابْتَلٰىهُ رَبُّهٗ

هٗ	رَبُّ	هٗ	مَاابْتَل	اِذَا	الْاِنْسَانُ	اَمَّا	فَ
his	Lord	him	tests	when	human	concerned	So far as

					being (is)		

15. So far as human being is concerned, when one’s Lord tests him/her and (thereby)…

فَأَكْرَمَهُ وَنَعَّمَهُ فَيَقُوْلُ رَبِّيٓ أَكْرَمَنِ ﴿١٥﴾

أَكْرَمَنِ	يِ	رَبِّ	قُوْلُ	فَ	هُ	نَعَّمَ	وَ	هُ	أَكْرَمَ	فَ
honored me	My	Lord	he says	so	him	Bless ed	and	him	honored	So

... honors and blesses one, he/she would (only) say ‘my Lord honored me!’

وَأَمَّآ إِذَا مَا ابْتَلٰهُ فَقَدَرَ عَلَيْهِ

هِ	عَلَيْ	قَدَرَ	فَ	هُ	مَا ابْتَلٰى	إِذَا	وَأَمَّآ
him	on	limits	and	him	He tests	when	And

16. And when God tests and thereby rations……

رِزْقَهُ فَيَقُوْلُ رَبِّيٓ أَهَانَنِ ﴿١٦﴾

أَهَانَنِ	يِ	رَبِّ	يَقُوْلُ	فَ	هُ	رِزْقَ
disgraced me	my	Lord	he says	So	his	provision

…….. one’s sustenance one would (only) say: ‘my Lord has disgraced me!’

كَلَّا بَلْ لَّا تُكْرِمُوْنَ الْيَتِيْمَ ﴿١٧﴾

الْيَتِيْمَ	تُكْرِمُوْنَ	لَّا	بَلْ	كَلَّا
the orphans	honor	(you) do not	rather	Nay

17. Nay, rather you do not honor the orphans!

وَلَا تَحٰٓضُّوْنَ عَلٰى طَعَامِ الْمِسْكِيْنِ ﴿١٨﴾

الْمِسْكِيْنِ	طَعَامِ	عَلٰى	تَحٰٓضُّوْنَ	لَا	وَ
the poor	feeding	on	Urge	(you) do not	and

18. And do not urge on the feeding of the poor!

وَتَأْكُلُوْنَ التُّرَاثَ أَكْلًا لَّمًّا ﴿١٩﴾

أَكْلًا لَّمًّا	التُّرَاثَ	تَأْكُلُوْنَ	وَ
devouring (it) altogeher	Inheritance	you devour	And

19. And you devour the inheritance, eating up all of it!

وَّتُحِبُّوْنَ الْمَالَ حُبًّا جَمًّا ﴿٢٠﴾

جَمًّا	حُبًّا	الْمَالَ	تُحِبُّوْنَ	وَّ
too much	loving (it)	the wealth	you love	And

20. And you love the wealth too much!

كَلَّآ إِذَا دُكَّتِ الْأَرْضُ دَكًّا دَكًّا ﴿٢١﴾

دَكًّا	دَكًّا	الْأَرْضُ	دُكَّتِ	إِذَا	كَلَّآ
(completely) flattened	(completely) flattened	the earth	is beaten	When	Nay

21. Nay, when earth is beaten down (and) is completely flattened.

وَّجَآءَ رَبُّكَ وَالْمَلَكُ صَفًّا صَفًّا ﴿٢٢﴾

صَفًّا	صَفًّا	الْمَلَكُ	وَ	كَ	رَبُّ	جَآءَ	وَّ
rank	rank (after)	the angels	and	your	Lord	arrives	And

22. And your Lord arrives, and the angels, rank after rank.

وَجِايْٓءَ يَوْمَئِذٍۭ بِجَهَنَّمَ ۙ يَوْمَئِذٍ يَّتَذَكَّرُ

يَّتَذَكَّرُ	يَوْمَئِذٍ	جَهَنَّمَ	بِ	يَوْمَئِذٍۭ	جِايْٓءَ	وَ
will receive reminding	that day	Hell	(with)	that day	(is) brought	And

23. And the Gehenna is brought (near) that day. That day, human being will receive the reminding,

الْإِنْسَانُ وَأَنّٰى لَهُ الذِّكْرٰى ﴿٢٣﴾

الذِّكْرٰى	هُ	لَ	أَنّٰى	وَ	الْإِنْسَانُ
the reminding	him/her	for	where is	but	human beings

but how shall the reminding be (beneficial) for him/her?

يَقُوْلُ يٰلَيْتَنِيْ قَدَّمْتُ لِحَيَاتِيْ ﴿٢٤﴾

ي	حَيَاتِ	لِ	قَدَّمْتُ	يٰلَيْتَنِيْ	يَقُوْلُ
my	(real) life	for	I had forwarded	Oh! would that	He will say

24. He/she will say, ‘Oh! Would that I had forwarded for my (real) life.

فَيَوْمَئِذٍ لَّا يُعَذِّبُ عَذَابَهٗٓ أَحَدٌ ﴿٢٥﴾

أَحَدٌ	هٗٓ	عَذَابَ	يُعَذِّبُ	لَّا	يَوْمَئِذٍ	فَ
any one	His	punishment	punish	does not	that day	So

25. So, the way God’s punishment will be that Day, no one (ever) punishes (any) one.

وَّلَا يُوْثِقُ وَثَاقَهٗٓ أَحَدٌ ﴿٢٦﴾

أَحَدٌ	هٗٓ	وَثَاقَ	يُوْثِقُ	لَا	وَّ

anyone	His	binding	binds (anyone)	no (one)	And

26. And no one (ever) binds (anyone), the way God shall bind (that Day)!

يَٰٓأَيَّتُهَا ٱلنَّفْسُ ٱلْمُطْمَئِنَّةُ ٢٧

ٱلْمُطْمَئِنَّةُ	ٱلنَّفْسُ	أَيَّتُهَا
Satisfied	Person	O!

27. O! (completely) satisfied person!
(Person having complete peace of mind and soul.)

ٱرْجِعِيٓ إِلَىٰ رَبِّكِ رَاضِيَةً مَّرْضِيَّةً ٢٨

مَّرْضِيَّةً	رَاضِيَةً	كِ	رَبِّ	إِلَىٰ	ٱرْجِعِيٓ
(He) is pleased with you	(you) are pleased with Him	your	Lord	To	Come back

28. Come back to your Lord! You are pleased (fully satisfied with your Lord) and (your Lord is) pleased with (you)!

فَٱدْخُلِي فِي عِبَٰدِي ٢٩

ي	عِبَٰدِ	فِي	ٱدْخُلِي	فَ
My	servants	Into	Enter	So

29. Enter into (the Company of) My servants.

وَٱدْخُلِي جَنَّتِي ٣٠

ي	جَنَّتِ	ٱدْخُلِي	وَ
My	Garden	enter	And

30. And enter into My Garden.

89 (c) Outline Structure of Sūrah al-Fajr

The *sūrah* makes its point in five stages:

A. **[*Āyāt* 1-5] underline some special (calm & quiet) moments.**
for remembrance of God, for seeking God's forgiveness as well as for reflecting upon Divine Signs……………..
(This will help their moral and spiritual development.)

B. **[*Āyāt* 6-13] derive a lesson from the history of human civilizations.**
Those who are so involved in the pursuit of this worldly pleasures that they do not spare any time to remember God's name, they develop a tendency to transgress against God. They create corruption in human society like the People of 'Ād, *Thamud* and Pharaoh.
When there is too much transgression, God takes action.

C. **[*Āyāt* 14-20] disucss the present situation.**
Today also, people are unconcerned with their duty toward alienated and deprived sections of human society. Everywhere there is exploitation, oppression and injustice.
People have no sense of accountability.

D. **[*Āyāt* 21-26] present a picture of the Day of Judgment.**
When the Hell is drawn closer, the criminal would cry:
'Would that I had sent forth for my (real) life!'

E. **[*Āyāt* 27-30] deal with the Divine Reception of the virtuous people.**
Fully satisfied with their reward, they will enjoy company of the virtuous servants of God - in the Vicinity of their Merciful God Who calls them 'My (beloved) servants!'

(They used the above peaceful moments in the remembrance of God and were concerned with their social obligations assigned to them from their Lord.)

89 (d) Sūrah al-Fajr
Understanding and Interpretation

The people should learn a lesson from the story of Human Civilization as recieved in the Qur'an. Consider the Divine Punishment which eliminted some earlier transgressors who corrupted the human society and did not correct their unjust ways in spite of repeated remindings from the prophets.

The well-off people who do not have any sense of accountability to God are so lost in the pursuit of immediate gains that they totally neglect their duties to other human beings. When a new world is created on The Judgment Day and the criminals see the Hell with their own eyes, then they will realize that the real life is the one that begins after death. Only in the Hereafter will the people understand that through the differences among people's financial status, God just wanted to see how those who have, would share or fail to share their resources with those who do not have.

According to *Sūrah al-Fajr* (89) the remedy of the above negligence lies in the remembrance of God and in making the use, for this purpose, of certain calm and quiet moments, more so on certain blessed nights.

In the Hereafter, God's beloved servants – who derived inner peace through their remembrance of God and who did not fail to do their duty to the alienated and deprived sections of sciety – will be welcome, in the Garden, in God's Vicinity and in the company of all virtuous people.

Chapter Nine

90 (a) Sūrah al-Balad

سُوۡرَةُ الۡبَلَدِ

بِسۡمِ اللّٰهِ الرَّحۡمٰنِ الرَّحِيۡمِ

لَآ اُقۡسِمُ بِهٰذَا الۡبَلَدِۙ ﴿١﴾ وَاَنۡتَ حِلٌّۢ بِهٰذَا الۡبَلَدِۙ ﴿٢﴾ وَوَالِدٍ وَّمَا
وَلَدَۙ ﴿٣﴾ لَقَدۡ خَلَقۡنَا الۡاِنۡسَانَ فِىۡ كَبَدٍؕ ﴿٤﴾ اَيَحۡسَبُ اَنۡ لَّنۡ
يَّقۡدِرَ عَلَيۡهِ اَحَدٌ ﴿٥﴾ يَقُوۡلُ اَهۡلَكۡتُ مَالًا لُّبَدًاؕ ﴿٦﴾ اَيَحۡسَبُ اَنۡ
لَّمۡ يَرَهٗۤ اَحَدٌؕ ﴿٧﴾ اَلَمۡ نَجۡعَلۡ لَّهٗ عَيۡنَيۡنِۙ ﴿٨﴾ وَلِسَانًا وَّشَفَتَيۡنِۙ ﴿٩﴾ وَ
هَدَيۡنٰهُ النَّجۡدَيۡنِۚ ﴿١٠﴾ فَلَا اقۡتَحَمَ الۡعَقَبَةَ ﴿١١﴾ وَمَاۤ اَدۡرٰٮكَ مَا
الۡعَقَبَةُؕ ﴿١٢﴾ فَكُّ رَقَبَةٍۙ ﴿١٣﴾ اَوۡ اِطۡعٰمٌ فِىۡ يَوۡمٍ ذِىۡ مَسۡغَبَةٍۙ ﴿١٤﴾
يَّتِيۡمًا ذَا مَقۡرَبَةٍۙ ﴿١٥﴾ اَوۡ مِسۡكِيۡنًا ذَا مَتۡرَبَةٍؕ ﴿١٦﴾ ثُمَّ كَانَ مِنَ
الَّذِيۡنَ اٰمَنُوۡا وَتَوَاصَوۡا بِالصَّبۡرِ وَتَوَاصَوۡا بِالۡمَرۡحَمَةِؕ ﴿١٧﴾ اُولٰٓـئِكَ
اَصۡحٰبُ الۡمَيۡمَنَةِؕ ﴿١٨﴾ وَالَّذِيۡنَ كَفَرُوۡا بِاٰيٰتِنَا هُمۡ اَصۡحٰبُ
الۡمَشۡئَمَةِؕ ﴿١٩﴾ عَلَيۡهِمۡ نَارٌ مُّؤۡصَدَةٌ ﴿٢٠﴾

90 (b) Word by word translation of Sūrah al-Balad

لَآ اُقْسِمُ بِهٰذَا الْبَلَدِ ۝١

الْبَلَدِ	هٰذَا	بِ	اُقْسِمُ	لَآ
city	this	By	I swear	No

1. No, I swear by this city;

وَاَنْتَ حِلٌّۢ بِهٰذَا الْبَلَدِ ۝٢

الْبَلَدِ	هٰذَا	بِ	حِلٌّۢ	اَنْتَ	وَ
city	this	In	(are) lawful	you	And

2. While you have been made lawful (hurting you is no crime) in this city.

وَوَالِدٍ وَّمَا وَلَدَ ۝٣

وَلَدَ	مَا	وَّ	وَالِدٍ	وَ
he begot	what	And	a father	By

3. I swear by a father and what he begot.

لَقَدْ خَلَقْنَا الْاِنْسَانَ فِيْ كَبَدٍ ۝٤

كَبَدٍ	فِيْ	الْاِنْسَانَ	خَلَقْنَا	لَقَدْ
hardship	in	the human	We have created	Surely

4. Surely, We have created human beings amidst hardship.

اَيَحْسَبُ اَنْ لَّنْ يَّقْدِرَ عَلَيْهِ اَحَدٌ ۝٥

اَحَدٌ	هِ	عَلَيْ	يَّقْدِرَ	لَّنْ	اَنْ	يَحْسَبُ	اَ
anyone	him	over	(have) power	does not	that	he think	Does

5. Does he think that no one has power over him?

يَقُوْلُ اَهْلَكْتُ مَالًا لُّبَدًا ۝٦

لُّبَدًا	مَالًا	اَهْلَكْتُ	يَقُوْلُ
piles (of)	wealth	I have squandered	He says

6. He says, 'I have squandered piles of wealth!'

اَيَحْسَبُ اَنْ لَّمْ يَرَهٗٓ اَحَدٌ ۝٧

اَحَدٌ	هٗٓ	يَرَ	لَّمْ	اَنْ	يَحْسَبُ	اَ
anyone	him	noticed	not	that	he think	Does

اَلَمۡ نَجۡعَلۡ لَّهٗ عَیۡنَیۡنِۙ ۸

عَیۡنَیۡنِ	هٗ	لَّ	نَجۡعَلۡ	لَمۡ	اَ
two eyes	him	For	We make	not	Did

8. Did We not make for him two eyes?

وَلِسَانًا وَّ شَفَتَیۡنِۙ ۹

شَفَتَیۡنِ	وَّ	لِسَانًا	وَ
two lips	And	a tongue	And

9. And a tongue and two lips?

وَ هَدَیۡنٰهُ النَّجۡدَیۡنِۚ ۱۰

النَّجۡدَیۡنِ	هٗ	هَدَیۡنٰ	وَ
two highways	him	We showed	And

10. And We showed him the two highways (doing good and avoiding evil).

فَلَا اقۡتَحَمَ الۡعَقَبَةَ ۱۱

الۡعَقَبَةَ	اقۡتَحَمَ	لَا	فَ
uphill (task)	strive	(he) did not	So

11. Yet he did not do the uphill task.

وَ مَاۤ اَدۡرٰىكَ مَا الۡعَقَبَةُ ۱۲

الۡعَقَبَةُ	مَا	كَ	اَدۡرٰ	مَاۤ	وَ
the uphill task	what (is)	you	make understand	what	And

12. And what will make you understand what the uphill task is?

فَكُّ رَقَبَةٍۙ ۱۳

رَقَبَةٍ	فَكُّ
a slave	Freeing

13. Freeing a slave (or a man in bondage),

اَوۡ اِطۡعٰمٌ فِیۡ یَوۡمٍ ذِیۡ مَسۡغَبَةٍۙ ۱۴

مَسۡغَبَةٍ	ذِیۡ	یَوۡمٍ	فِیۡ	اِطۡعٰمٌ	اَوۡ
famine	of	a day	on	feeding	Or

14. Or feeding, on a day of famine,

يَّتِيْمًا ذَا مَقْرَبَةٍ ۱۵

مَقْرَبَةٍ	ذَا	يَّتِيْمًا
closely related	who is	An orphan

15. An orphan who is closely related,

اَوْ مِسْكِيْنًا ذَا مَتْرَبَةٍ ۱۶

مَتْرَبَةٍ	ذَا	مِسْكِيْنًا	اَوْ
downtrodden	who is	a poor	Or

16. Or a poor person who is downtrodden.

ثُمَّ كَانَ مِنَ الَّذِيْنَ اٰمَنُوْا وَ تَوَاصَوْا

تَوَاصَوْا	وَ	اٰمَنُوْا	الَّذِيْنَ	مِنَ	كَانَ	ثُمَّ
enjoined	and	who believed	those	among	he became	Then

17. Then he joined the community of believers, and enjoined

بِالصَّبْرِ وَ تَوَاصَوْا بِالْمَرْحَمَةِ ۱۷

الْمَرْحَمَةِ	بِ	تَوَاصَوْا	وَ	الصَّبْرِ	بِ
compassion	(with)	enjoined	And	steadfastness	(with)

steadfastness and enjoined compassion.

اُولٰٓئِكَ اَصْحٰبُ الْمَيْمَنَةِ ۱۸

الْمَيْمَنَةِ	اَصْحٰبُ	اُولٰٓئِكَ
(of) the good omen	(are) the people	Those

18. Those are the People of the Right Hand.

وَ الَّذِيْنَ كَفَرُوْا بِاٰيٰتِنَا هُمْ اَصْحٰبُ الْمَشْئَمَةِ ۱۹

الْمَشْئَمَةِ	اَصْحٰبُ	هُمْ	نَا	اٰيٰتِ	بِ	كَفَرُوْ	الَّذِيْنَ	وَ
(of) the bad omen	(are) the people	they	Our	signs	With	disbelived	those who	And

19. And those who disbelieved Our Signs, they are the People of the Left Hand (the people with bad omen).

عَلَيْهِمْ نَارٌ مُّؤْصَدَةٌ ۲۰

مُّؤْصَدَةٌ	نَارٌ	هِمْ	عَلَي
closed	(is) a fire	them	Over

20. They shall have a Fire, closed over them.

90 (c) Outline Structure of Sūrah al-Balad

The *sūrah* makes its point in five stages:

A. **[*Āyāt* 1-4]** The *āyāt* of *qasam* (swearing) call our attention to the present striving in the sacred city of Makkah, which is related with the opposition to the Qur'anic Movement, as well as some earlier strivings - those by Adam and his Children or more recently by Abraham and his Children. **Humans are, by their very nature, hard-working.**

B. **[*Āyāt* 5–7]** underline those whose strivings express a tendency to become **arrogant and morally irresponsible**.

[*Āyāt* 8–10] comment: this is the state of affairs, in spite of the fact that God has also given to humans:

ability to see and learn lessons from what they see
ability to communicate and tell others if there is some danger ahead
and moral consciousness.

D. **[*Āyāt* 11–17]** present admirable striving in two steps:
[*Āyāt* 11-16] deal with the strivings of the virtuous people
[*Āyah* 17] states: the same people join the believing community and then continue their striving through it.

E. **[*Āyāt* 18–20]** The concluding *āyāt* state:

in the Hereafter, what difference will make

the striving of the believers

and that of their opponents.

90 (d) Sūrah al-Balad
Understanding and Interpretation

Presenting as its witness the striving that is going on against the Qur'anic Movement in the otherwise Secure (Holy) City of Makkah, where Abraham and Ishmael built *Masjid al Ḥarām* as the center of their *tawḥīdic* striving, the *sūrah* affirms that humans are very hard working by their very nature. However, quite often they are very extravagant and arrogant. They forget that they are accountable to God, Who is watching them all the time.

This is the situation in spite of the fact that God blessed them with the ability to make a conscientious judgment and distinguish right from wrong.

However, there are people who do the right kind of striving - those who work for the welfare of human society; e.g., they work for the liberation of slaves and those fellow humans who are in some kind of bondage. They help down-trodden and alienated sections of human society – starting from those who are closely related with them and more so during the times of adversity.

The above are the people who would join the Community of Believers (and then they will work through it in the path of virtue). They will remind each other of their mutual duties and give moral support to each other, e.g., when they face problems in the way of their mission. These are the blessed people who will enter into the Paradise.

Those who have violently rejected the Qur'anic call are, essentially, the people who lack generosity. These people will enter the Hell, whose Fire will be closed upon them. These are unblessed people.

Chapter Ten

91 (a) Sūrah ash-Shams

سُوْرَةُ الشَّمْسِ

بِسْمِ اللّٰهِ الرَّحْمٰنِ الرَّحِيْمِ

وَالشَّمْسِ وَضُحٰهَا (١) وَالْقَمَرِ اِذَا تَلٰهَا (٢) وَالنَّهَارِ اِذَا جَلّٰهَا (٣) وَ

الَّيْلِ اِذَا يَغْشٰهَا (٤) وَالسَّمَآءِ وَمَا بَنٰهَا (٥) وَالْاَرْضِ وَمَا طَحٰهَا (٦)

وَنَفْسٍ وَّمَا سَوّٰهَا (٧) فَاَلْهَمَهَا فُجُوْرَهَا وَتَقْوٰهَا (٨) قَدْ اَفْلَحَ مَنْ

زَكّٰهَا (٩) وَقَدْ خَابَ مَنْ دَسّٰهَا (١٠) كَذَّبَتْ ثَمُوْدُ بِطَغْوٰهَآ (١١) اِذِ انْۢبَعَثَ

اَشْقٰهَا (١٢) فَقَالَ لَهُمْ رَسُوْلُ اللّٰهِ نَاقَةَ اللّٰهِ وَسُقْيٰهَا (١٣) فَكَذَّبُوْهُ

فَعَقَرُوْهَا فَدَمْدَمَ عَلَيْهِمْ رَبُّهُمْ بِذَنْۢبِهِمْ فَسَوّٰهَا (١٤) وَلَا يَخَافُ عُقْبٰهَا (١٥)

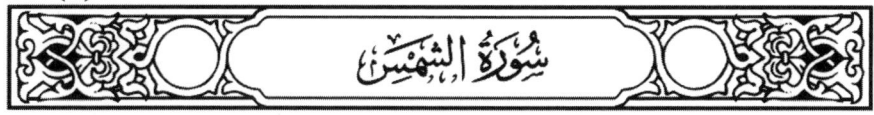

91 (b) Word by word translation of Sūrah Ash-Shams

وَالشَّمْسِ وَضُحٰىهَا ۝١

ـهَا	ضُحٰى	وَ	الشَّمْسِ	وَ
its	brightness(at forenoon)	and	the sun	By

1. By the sun and its brightness (at forenoon),

وَالْقَمَرِ اِذَا تَلٰىهَا ۝٢

ـهَا	تَلٰى	اِذَا	الْقَمَرِ	وَ
it	it followed	when	the moon	By

2. By the moon when it follows it,

وَالنَّهَارِ اِذَا جَلّٰىهَا ۝٣

ـهَا	جَلّٰى	اِذَا	النَّهَارِ	وَ
it	it makes bright	when	the day	By

3. By day when it (sun) makes it bright.

وَالَّيْلِ اِذَا يَغْشٰىهَا ۝٤

ـهَا	يَغْشٰى	اِذَا	الَّيْلِ	وَ
it	it covers	when	the night	By

4. By the night when it covers it (sun).

وَالسَّمَآءِ وَمَا بَنٰىهَا ۝٥

ـهَا	بَنٰى	مَا	وَ	السَّمَآءِ	وَ
it (is)	Built	the way	and	The Heaven	By

I. By the heaven and the way it is built (its wonderful building),

وَالْاَرْضِ وَمَا طَحٰىهَا ۝٦

ـهَا	طَحٰى	مَا	وَ	الْاَرْضِ	وَ
it (is)	spread	the way	and	The Earth	By

6. By the earth and the way it is spread out, made livable.

وَنَفْسٍ وَّمَا سَوّٰىهَا ﴿٧﴾

هَا	سَوّٰى	مَا	وَّ	نَفْسٍ	وَ
it	(is) perfected	the way	and	a self	By

7. By a self (an individual human being) and the way it is perfected.

فَاَلْهَمَهَا فُجُوْرَهَا وَتَقْوٰىهَا ﴿٨﴾

هَا	تَقْوٰى	وَ	هَا	فُجُوْرَ	هَا	اَلْهَمَ	فَ
its	piety	and	its	wickedness	it	inspir ed	So

8. And thus (God) inspired it with (the consciousness of) what is wicked and what is pious.

قَدْ اَفْلَحَ مَنْ زَكّٰىهَا ﴿٩﴾

هَا	زَكّٰى	مَنْ	اَفْلَحَ	قَدْ
his/her	took care of (his/her) spiritual and moral development	one who	achieved success	Surely

9. That person has achieved *Falāḥ* (Ultimate Happiness/Success) who took care of one's own spiritual and moral development (did one's own *tazkiyah*)

وَقَدْ خَابَ مَنْ دَسّٰىهَا ﴿١٠﴾

هَا	دَسّٰى	مَنْ	خَابَ	قَدْ	وَ
it	spoiled	one who	is doomed	surely	And

10. That person is doomed who spoiled it (his own self).

كَذَّبَتْ ثَمُوْدُ بِطَغْوٰىهَا ﴿١١﴾

هَا	طَغْوٰى	بِ	ثَمُوْدُ	كَذَّبَتْ
their	transgression	due to	Thamud	Gave a lie

11. Due to their transgression, Thamūd gave a lie (to their prophet).

اِذِ انْۢبَعَثَ اَشْقٰىهَا ﴿١٢﴾

هَا	اَشْقٰى	انْۢبَعَثَ	اِذِ
their	worst wretch (of)	Uprose	When

12. Think of the time when the worst wretch among them uprose!

فَقَالَ لَهُمْ رَسُوْلُ اللّٰهِ نَاقَةَ اللّٰهِ وَ سُقْيٰهَا ﴿١٣﴾

ـهَا	سُقْيٰ	وَ	اللّٰهِ	نَاقَةَ	اللّٰهِ	رَسُوْلُ	هُمْ	لَ	قَالَ	فَ
her	drinking	and	(of) Allah	take care of the she -camel	(of) Allah	messenger	The m	To	said	So

13. So, the messenger of God said to them 'Take care of God's She-Camel and her drinking!'

فَكَذَّبُوْهُ فَعَقَرُوْهَا فَدَمْدَمَ

دَمْدَمَ	فَ	هَا	عَقَرُو	فَ	هُ	كَذَّبُوs	فَ
utterly destroyed	and	her	hamstrung	thereby	to him	they gave lie	So

14. So they gave lie to him (and) thereby killed the she-camel, therefore,..

عَلَيْهِمْ رَبُّهُمْ بِذَنْۢبِهِمْ فَسَوّٰىهَا ﴿١٤﴾

ـهَا	سَوّٰى	فَ	هِمْ	ذَنْۢبِ	بِ	هُمْ	رَبُّ	هِمْ	عَلَيْ
them	leveled	so	their	sin	due to	their	Lord	them	On

their Lord let loose His scourge upon them due to their sin and razed their city to the ground.

وَلَا يَخَافُ عُقْبٰهَا ﴿١٥﴾

ـهَا	عُقْبٰ	يَخَافُ	لَا	وَ
their	end result	(God) fear	does not	And

15. And He does not fear (what is going to be) their (fate in the) Hereafter.

91 (c) Outline Structure of Sūrah Ash-Shams

This *sūrah* makes its point in four stages:

A. **[*Āyāt* 1-8] present the perspective for the following sections:**
1-2 See the Sun – the primary source of light,
[The Revealed Guidance in Divine Words e.g. the Qur'an]
which is followed by the Moon
[The Guidance explained in human words].
3-4 The day radiates light of Sun, the night only covers it.
5-8 See the strong build of the Astronomical World.
Consider Earth and how it is made livable for humans.
Consider the most advanced creature - being of a human,
with the consciousness of good and evil.

B. **[*Āyāt* 9-10] ultimately 'who attains *Salvation?*':**
One, who takes care of one's own *tazkiyah* attains *Falāḥ*.
Whoever does not care for one's own self is ruined.

C. **[*Āyāt* 11-14] deal with the example of *Thamūd.***
Due to their transgression,
Thamūd violently rejected the call of their prophet
who was inviting them to take care of their *tazkiyah* .
Imagine: when most wretched leadership developed in this nation!
So their messenger said to them:
Take care of God's She-Camel and its drinking!
They violently rejected him and slaughtered her.
So the Divine Punishment eliminated them.

D. **[*Āyāt* 15] state, in the Hereafter too, their Merciful God would not mind their having a severe punishment.**

91 (d) Sūrah Ash-Shams
Understanding and Interpretation

Sūrah ash-Shams (91) continues the discussion of *tazkiyah* which was introduced in *Sūrah al- 'A'lā* (87). It underlines the need of an individual's initiative for one's own self-purification as well as spiritual and moral growth (*tazkiyah*), which is the key to one's *Falāḥ*.

Humankind has great potential for spiritual and moral progress. It is due to this that it occupies a unique place in the world of creation. *Sūrah Ash-Shams* (91) focuses on the role of the Revealed Divine Guidance, in enlightening the human self. However, it works only when a person is inclined to receive benefit, takes care of one's own *tazkiyah*, and follows the guidance of the Prophet.

The *sūrah* makes an interesting concluding remark: God who perfected the creation of every person (*nafs*) also knows how to take care of the spiritual progress of the communities of human beings. When Thamud became spiritually rotten – they even killed the Great Divine Sign i.e. The She-Camel of God – Divine Punishment eliminated them from the surface of the earth. This was necesary for the moral and spiritual growth (*tazkiyah*) of the rest of humankind.

And, in the Hereafter too when after being alienated from the rest of humanity, this rotten part of its body is thrown into the Hellfire, God will not mind their receiving such a severe punishment.

Chapter Eleven

92 (a) Sūrah al-Layl

سُوْرَةُ اللَّيْلِ

بِسْمِ اللّٰهِ الرَّحْمٰنِ الرَّحِيْمِ

وَالَّيْلِ إِذَا يَغْشٰى ﴿١﴾ وَالنَّهَارِ إِذَا تَجَلّٰى ﴿٢﴾ وَمَا خَلَقَ الذَّكَرَ

وَالْأُنْثٰى ﴿٣﴾ إِنَّ سَعْيَكُمْ لَشَتّٰى ﴿٤﴾ فَأَمَّا مَنْ أَعْطٰى وَاتَّقٰى ﴿٥﴾ وَصَدَّقَ

بِالْحُسْنٰى ﴿٦﴾ فَسَنُيَسِّرُهٗ لِلْيُسْرٰى ﴿٧﴾ وَأَمَّا مَنْ بَخِلَ وَاسْتَغْنٰى ﴿٨﴾ وَ

كَذَّبَ بِالْحُسْنٰى ﴿٩﴾ فَسَنُيَسِّرُهٗ لِلْعُسْرٰى ﴿١٠﴾ وَمَا يُغْنِيْ عَنْهُ مَالُهٗٓ إِذَا

تَرَدّٰى ﴿١١﴾ إِنَّ عَلَيْنَا لَلْهُدٰى ﴿١٢﴾ وَإِنَّ لَنَا لَلْاٰخِرَةَ وَالْأُوْلٰى ﴿١٣﴾ فَأَنْذَرْ

تُكُمْ نَارًا تَلَظّٰى ﴿١٤﴾ لَا يَصْلٰىهَآ إِلَّا الْأَشْقَى ﴿١٥﴾ الَّذِيْ كَذَّبَ وَتَوَلّٰى ﴿١٦﴾ وَ

سَيُجَنَّبُهَا الْأَتْقَى ﴿١٧﴾ الَّذِيْ يُؤْتِيْ مَالَهٗ يَتَزَكّٰى ﴿١٨﴾ وَمَا لِأَحَدٍ عِنْدَهٗ مِنْ

نِّعْمَةٍ تُجْزٰٓى ﴿١٩﴾ إِلَّا ابْتِغَآءَ وَجْهِ رَبِّهِ الْأَعْلٰى ﴿٢٠﴾ وَلَسَوْفَ يَرْضٰى ﴿٢١﴾

92 (b) Word by word translation of Sūrah al-Layl

وَالَّيْلِ اِذَا يَغْشٰى ١

يَغْشٰى	اِذَا	الَّيْلِ	وَ
it prevails	when	the night	By

1. By the night when it prevails.

وَالنَّهَارِ اِذَا تَجَلّٰى ٢

تَجَلّٰى	اِذَا	النَّهَارِ	وَ
it shines	when	the day	By

2. By the day when it shines.

وَمَا خَلَقَ الذَّكَرَ وَالْاُنْثٰٓى ٣

الْاُنْثٰٓى	وَ	الذَّكَرَ	خَلَقَ	مَا	وَ
female	and	Male	creation (of)	(the very)	By

3. By the creation of male and female,

اِنَّ سَعْيَكُمْ لَشَتّٰى ٤

شَتّٰى	لَ	كُمْ	سَعْيَ	اِنَّ
(are) diversified	surely	Your	effort(s)	Verily

4. Verily, your efforts are diversified (they go in various directions).

فَاَمَّا مَنْ اَعْطٰى وَاتَّقٰى ٥

اتَّقٰى	وَ	اَعْطٰى	مَنْ	اَمَّا	فَ
observed *taqwā*	and	gave	one who	so for as	So

5. So far as that person is concerned who gives and observes *taqwā*.

وَصَدَّقَ بِالْحُسْنٰى ٦

الْحُسْنٰى	بِ	صَدَّقَ	وَ
al-Ḥusnā	To	testified	And

6. And testifies to *al-Husnā* (the most beautiful path to which the Qur'an is calling).

فَسَنُيَسِّرُهٗ لِلْيُسْرٰى ۝٧

اَلْيُسْرٰى	لِ	هٗ	نُيَسِّرُ	سَ	فَ
easy journey	For	him/her	we shall prepare	(soon)	Therefore

7. Therefore, we shall prepare him for the Easy Journey.

وَاَمَّا مَنْۢ بَخِلَ وَاسْتَغْنٰى ۝٨

اسْتَغْنٰى	وَ	بَخِلَ	مَنْ	اَمَّا	وَ
had no sense of responsibility	and	acted niggardly	who	so far as (that person is concerned)	And

8. And so far as the niggardly person is concerned who has no sense of responsibility,

وَكَذَّبَ بِالْحُسْنٰى ۝٩

الْحُسْنٰى	بِ	كَذَّبَ	وَ
al-Husnā	To	gave lie	And (thereby)

9. And who (thereby) gives lie to *al-Husnā*,

فَسَنُيَسِّرُهٗ لِلْعُسْرٰى ۝١٠

الْعُسْرٰى	لِ	هٗ	نُيَسِّرُ	سَ	فَ
the *Journey of Hardship*	For	him/her	we shall prepare	(soon)	Therefore

10. Therefore, we shall prepare him/her for the Journey of Hardship.

وَمَا يُغْنِيْ عَنْهُ مَالُهٗۤ اِذَا تَرَدّٰى ۝١١

تَرَدّٰى	اِذَا	هٗ	مَالُ	هٗ	عَنْ	يُغْنِيْ	مَا		وَ
(he) is ruined	when	his	Wealth	him	for	benefit	(will) not		And

1. And when he/she is ruined his/her wealth will not benefit him/her.

اِنَّ عَلَيْنَا لَلْهُدٰى ۝١٢

الْهُدٰى	لَ	نَا	عَلَيْ	اِنَّ
The Guidance	(surely) is	Us	upon	Verily

12. Verily, We have taken the responsibility that We shall guide.

وَاِنَّ لَنَا لَلْاٰخِرَةَ وَالْاُوْلٰى ۝١٣

الْاُوْلٰى	وَ	الْاٰخِرَةَ	لَ	نَا	لَ	اِنَّ	وَ
first life	and	hereafter	(surely)	Us	belong to	verily	And

13. And verily, the Hereafter as well as the first creation belongs to Us.

فَأَنذَرْتُكُمْ نَارًا تَلَظَّىٰ ﴿١٤﴾

تَلَظَّىٰ	نَارًا	كُمْ	أَنذَرْتُ	فَ
blazed	(of) fire	(to) you	I gave warning	Therefore

14. Therefore, I warn you of a blazing fire.

لَا يَصْلَاهَا إِلَّا الْأَشْقَى ﴿١٥﴾

الْأَشْقَى	إِلَّا	هَا	يَصْلَى	لَا
most wretched person	except	(in) it	will roast	None

15. None but the most wretched person will roast in it;

الَّذِي كَذَّبَ وَتَوَلَّىٰ ﴿١٦﴾

تَوَلَّىٰ	وَ	كَذَّبَ	الَّذِي
turned away	and	violently rejected	Who

16. Who violently rejects My call to believe and turns away.

وَسَيُجَنَّبُهَا الْأَتْقَى ﴿١٧﴾

الْأَتْقَى	هَا	يُجَنَّبُ	سَ	وَ
the most God-fearing	It	be kept away from	(will)	And

17. And will be kept away from it the most God-fearing (the most responsible person).

الَّذِي يُؤْتِي مَالَهُ يَتَزَكَّىٰ ﴿١٨﴾

يَتَزَكَّىٰ	هُ	مَالَ	يُؤْتِي	الَّذِي
(seeking) own *tazkiyah*	his/her	Wealth	gave	Who

18. Who gives his/her wealth, seeking his/her own *tazkiyah*

وَمَا لِأَحَدٍ عِندَهُ مِن نِّعْمَةٍ تُجْزَىٰ ﴿١٩﴾

تُجْزَىٰ	نِّعْمَةٍ	مِن	هُ	عِندَ	أَحَدٍ	لِ	مَا	وَ
to be rewarded	blessin g	any	Him	accoding to	anyone	for /with	there is not	And

19. And according to him/her, none else has any blessing to give (to him/her) in reward.

إِلَّا ابْتِغَآءَ وَجْهِ رَبِّهِ الْأَعْلَىٰ ﴿٢٠﴾

الْأَعْلَىٰ	هِ	رَبِّ	وَجْهِ	ابْتِغَآءَ	إِلَّا
The Most High	(of) his	Lord	is the countenance	seeking	All (he is)

20. All he/she is seeking is the pleasure (the Countenance) of his/her Lord, The Most High.

وَلَسَوْفَ يَرْضَىٰ ﴿٢١﴾

يَرْضَىٰ	سَوْفَ	لَ	وَ
he will be pleased	(soon)	surely	And

21. And soon he/she will be pleased.

92 (c) Outline Structure of Sūrah al-Layl

A. **[*Āyāt* 1-3] Invite reflection over three realities:**

(i) The night when it prevails,
(ii) The day when it shines,
(iii) The creation of male and female.

B. **[*Āyāt* 4–10] The above is an evidence for the following**:

***Āyah* 4 'Human efforts are diversified'.**
***Āyāt* 5–7 Those who are prepared for the easy journey:**
who share in the needs of others,
and who live a socially responsible life,
and thereby testify beautiful teachings of the Book,
***Āyāt* 8-10 Those who are prepared for the difficult journey:**
those who lack generosity,
who are socially irresponsible,
and stand in opposition to the Qur'anic Movement.

C. **[*Āyāt* 11-13] connect section (B) with section (D)**

***Āyah* 11** states the fact that the second category of the people believe in wealth and not in God.
***Āyah* 12**: God has taken up the responsibility of guiding God's servants so God is sending these revelations.
***Āyah* 13**: This world as well as Hereafter is in God's Hand.

D. **[*Āyāt* 14-21] contain the concluding remark:**
Āyāt (14-16) Those who will be punished in the Hereafter.
Āyāt (17-21) God's loving /beloved servants.

92 (d) Sūrah al-Layl

Understanding and Interpretation

Sūrah Ash-Shams (91) explained that some people are like day. They shine in the light of Divine Guidance. The example of the other category of people is that of night which covers the light of the Sun. The *Sūrah al-Layl* (92) goes deeper into the root causes of the two conducts. The second category loves wealth and neglects the Hereafter. The first kind loves God and does its duty selflessly. These people are concerned with their moral and spiritual development (*tazkiyah*). They look for the pleasure of their Lord. And they will have it.

Life is an on-going journey. It continues after death. Possibly, the latter part of one's journey is a life in Paradise. *Sūrah al-Layl* calls it *Yusrā* (Easy Journey). Or it is a life in Hell or '*Usrā* (Difficult Journey). It is expected that those who have a responsible attitude in life and share their wealth with the needy will join the Qur'anic Movement. These are the people whom God will prepare for the Easy Journey. On the other hand, morally irresponsible persons who are unconcerned with their duty to the downtrodden and alienated people will stand in violent opposition to the Revealed Guidance. They are being prepared for *al-'Usra.*

The sūrah underlines, in the above perspective, that God has taken two tasks upon Himself:

1. God sends down Guidance for the benefit of His servants.

2. Later, God will create another world to judge and reward human actions in the light of the Divine Guidance.

Chapter Twelve

93 (a) Sūrah aḍ- Ḍuḥā

سُورَةُ الضُّحٰى

بِسْمِ اللّٰهِ الرَّحْمٰنِ الرَّحِيْمِ

وَالضُّحٰى ﴿١﴾ وَالَّيْلِ اِذَا سَجٰى ﴿٢﴾ مَا وَدَّعَكَ رَبُّكَ وَمَا قَلٰى ﴿٣﴾
وَلَلْاٰخِرَةُ خَيْرٌ لَّكَ مِنَ الْاُوْلٰى ﴿٤﴾ وَلَسَوْفَ يُعْطِيْكَ رَبُّكَ
فَتَرْضٰى ﴿٥﴾ اَلَمْ يَجِدْكَ يَتِيْمًا فَاٰوٰى ﴿٦﴾ وَوَجَدَكَ ضَآلًّا فَهَدٰى ﴿٧﴾
وَوَجَدَكَ عَآئِلًا فَاَغْنٰى ﴿٨﴾ فَاَمَّا الْيَتِيْمَ فَلَا تَقْهَرْ ﴿٩﴾ وَاَمَّا السَّآئِلَ
فَلَا تَنْهَرْ ﴿١٠﴾ وَاَمَّا بِنِعْمَةِ رَبِّكَ فَحَدِّثْ ﴿١١﴾

93 (b) Word by word translation of Sūrah Aḍ- Ḍuḥā

وَالضُّحٰىۙ ١

الضُّحٰى	وَ
the forenoon (bright hours)	By

1. By the bright forenoon hours.

وَالَّيۡلِ اِذَا سَجٰىۙ ٢

سَجٰى	اِذَا	الَّيۡلِ	وَ
all is still.	when	the night	By

2. By the night when all is still.

مَا وَدَّعَكَ رَبُّكَ وَمَا قَلٰىؕ ٣

قَلٰى	مَا	وَ	كَ	رَبُّ	كَ	وَدَّعَ	مَا
(He is) displeased with you	nor	(and)	your	Lord	you	has forsaken	Neither

3. Your Lord has not forsaken you, nor is He displeased with you.

وَلَلۡاٰخِرَةُ خَيۡرٌ لَّكَ مِنَ الۡاُوۡلٰىؕ ٤

الۡاُوۡلٰى	مِنَ	كَ	لَّ	خَيۡرٌ	اٰخِرَةُ	ال	لَ	وَ
ealier part	than	you	for	(is) better	later part	the	sure	And

4. And the later part of your life is better than the earlier part.

وَلَسَوۡفَ يُعۡطِيۡكَ رَبُّكَ فَتَرۡضٰىؕ ٥

تَرۡضٰى	فَ	كَ	رَبُّ	كَ	يُعۡطِيۡ	سَوۡفَ	لَ	وَ
you will be pleased	so	your	Lord	you	will give	soon	surely	And

5. And soon your Lord will give you and you will be (fully) pleased.

اَلَمۡ يَجِدۡكَ يَتِيۡمًا فَاٰوٰى ٦

اٰوٰى	فَ	يَتِيۡمًا	كَ	يَجِدۡ	لَمۡ	اَ
sheltered you	so	an orphan	you	God find	not	Did

6. Did (God) not find you an orphan and sheltered you?

وَوَجَدَكَ ضَآلًّا فَهَدٰى ٧

هَدٰى	فَ	ضَآلًّا	كَ	وَجَدَ	وَ
guided you	so	lost	you	God found	And

7. And (God) found you lost, so God guided you!

وَوَجَدَكَ عَآئِلًا فَاَغْنٰى ﴿٨﴾

اَغْنٰى	فَ	عَآئِلًا	كَ	وَجَدَ	وَ
made (you) rich	so	destitute	you	God found	And

8. And found you destitute, so (God) made you rich.

فَاَمَّا الْيَتِيْمَ فَلَا تَقْهَرْ ﴿٩﴾

تَقْهَرْ	لَا	فَ	الْيَتِيْمَ	اَمَّا	فَ
be harsh (with him)	do not	so	the orphan is concerned	so far as	Therefore

9. Therefore, so far as the orphan is concerned, do not be harsh with him.

وَاَمَّا السَّآئِلَ فَلَا تَنْهَرْ ﴿١٠﴾

تَنْهَرْ	لَا	فَ	السَّآئِلَ	اَمَّا	وَ
scold (him)	do not	so	one who asks for help	so far as (is concerned)	And

10. And one who asks for help, do not push him away

وَاَمَّا بِنِعْمَةِ رَبِّكَ فَحَدِّثْ ﴿١١﴾

حَدِّثْ	فَ	كَ	رَبِّ	نِعْمَةِ	بِ	اَمَّا	وَ
relate it	so	your	Lord	the Blessing of	(is concerned)	so far as	And

11. And so far as the Blessing (Guidance) of your Lord is concerned, relate it (to others).

93 (c) Outline Structure of Sūrah Aḍ- Ḍuḥā

The *sūrah* makes its point in four stages:

A. [*Āyah* 1 & 2] The Guidance has to reach out everywhere:

The *qasam* (swearing) diverts addressees' attention to the reality that darkness still covers the human world.

[The humanity is going to receive lot of good from the Prophetic Movement which has all the Divine support with it.]

B. [*Āyāt* 3-5] reassure the Prophet that God is with him:

O Prophet, be sure, your Lord has not forsaken you,
Nor is God displeased with you!
And you will continue making progress (in God's way).
God will give you more and more so you shall be fully satisfied.

C. [*Āyāt* 6-8] The favor, God has been doing to the Prophet:

You were an orphan, God gave you protection.
You were lost (i.e. you were looking for guidance),
God blessed you with the Guidance.
You were financially broken, God made you rich.

D. [*Āyāt* 9–11] Therefore, you also should:

Neither be harsh with the orphans,
Nor repulse the one who asks for help.
And so far as this Blessing (of Guidance)
is concerned, relate it to others.

93 (d) Sūrah Aḍ- Ḍuḥā
Understanding and Interpretation

The *sūrah* underlines that the Prophet has a very special status near God. It is due to the importance and significance of his *mission.* There is darkness everywhere in the world, and it is through the Prophet that God will bring the light. What is important: **This light has to reach its fullness** (its *ḍuḥā*).

The Prophet should not be worried on any unusual delay in the coming of a new installment of revelation. There may be some wisdom behind this delay.

The *sūrah* explains what actually the Prophetic mission is: Building up human beings's relationship with God by calling human beings to be thankful to their Lord. They should do their mutual duties to each other as servants of One God, and do their duty to God Himself, remembering him more and more.

Due to *sūrah's* special interest in the personality of the Prophet, the above point is explained through Prophet's own story. God has been closely watching his personal situation. Whenever, the Prophet needed Divine Help, it was there! As God's thankful servant, now it is his duty to be concerned with other servants of God - mainly with those who are alienated or in need of some help.

The *sūrah* concludes: To do his thanksgiving to his Master for The Blessing of Guidance, the Prophet should share this Divine Gift to the people - convey the *tawḥīdic* message to everyone.

Chapter Thirteen

94 (a) Sūrah ash-Sharḥ

سُوْرَةُ الشَّرْحِ

بِسْمِ اللّٰهِ الرَّحْمٰنِ الرَّحِيْمِ

بِسْمِ اللّٰهِ الرَّحْمٰنِ الرَّحِيْمِ

اَلَمْ نَشْرَحْ لَكَ صَدْرَكَ ﴿١﴾ وَوَضَعْنَا عَنْكَ وِزْرَكَ ﴿٢﴾ الَّذِيْٓ اَنْقَضَ
ظَهْرَكَ ﴿٣﴾ وَرَفَعْنَا لَكَ ذِكْرَكَ ﴿٤﴾ فَاِنَّ مَعَ الْعُسْرِ يُسْرًا ﴿٥﴾ اِنَّ مَعَ
الْعُسْرِ يُسْرًا ﴿٦﴾ فَاِذَا فَرَغْتَ فَانْصَبْ ﴿٧﴾ وَاِلٰى رَبِّكَ فَارْغَبْ ﴿٨﴾

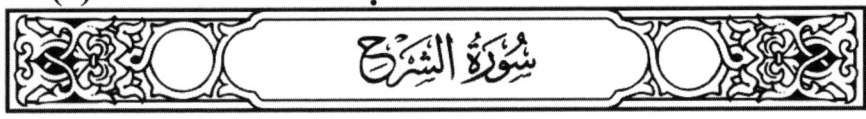

94 (b) Word by word translation of Sūrah Ash-Sharḥ

أَلَمْ نَشْرَحْ لَكَ صَدْرَكَ ۝١

كَ	صَدْرَ	كَ	لَ	نَشْرَحْ	لَمْ	أَ
your	breast	you	for	We expand	not	Did

1. Did we not expand your breast for you (i.e. opened your heart)

وَوَضَعْنَا عَنكَ وِزْرَكَ ۝٢

كَ	وِزْرَ	كَ	عَنْ	وَضَعْنَا	وَ
your	burden	you	from	We lifted	And

2. And We lifted your burden from you.

الَّذِيٓ أَنقَضَ ظَهْرَكَ ۝٣

كَ	ظَهْرَ	أَنقَضَ	الَّذِيٓ
your	back	weighed down	That

3. That weighed down upon your back (to its breaking point).

وَرَفَعْنَا لَكَ ذِكْرَكَ ۝٤

كَ	ذِكْرَ	كَ	لَ	رَفَعْنَا	وَ
your	remembrance	you	for	We raised high	And

4. And We raised high for you, your remembrance (i.e. your dhikr of God).

فَإِنَّ مَعَ الْعُسْرِ يُسْرًا ۝٥

يُسْرًا	الْعُسْرِ	مَعَ	إِنَّ	فَ
an ease	the hardship is	with	verily	So

5. So verily, with the hardship (comes) an ease.

إِنَّ مَعَ الْعُسْرِ يُسْرًا ۝٦

يُسْرًا	الْعُسْرِ	مَعَ	إِنَّ
an ease	the hardship is	with	verily

6. Verily, with the hardship (comes) an ease.

فَإِذَا فَرَغْتَ فَانصَبْ ۝٧

انصَبْ	فَ	فَرَغْتَ	إِذَا	فَ

toil	so (still)	you are relieved	when	Therefore
7. Therefore, when you are relieved (from your mission), still toil (at the remembrance of God and ṣalāh).				

وَاِلٰى رَبِّكَ فَارْغَبْ ﴿٨﴾					
ارْغَبْ	فَ	كَ	رَبِّ	اِلٰى	وَ
turn in devotion	so	your	Lord	to	And
8. And thereby turn to your Lord in devotion.					

94 (c) Outline Structure of Sūrah Ash-Sharḥ

The *sūrah* makes its point in three stages:

A. **[*Āyāt* 1-4] explain how God has been helping the Prophet during his striving for the *tawḥīdic* mission.**

Āyah 1: Is it not the case that God opened your chest?
Āyah 2 & *āyah* 3: And made, the burden (of work) that was breaking your back, light.
Āyah 4: God raised high, the glorification *(dhikr)* of your Lord, that you initiated.

B. **[*Āyah* 5 and *āyah* 6] explain that the Prophet's task became so easy due to his following the policy of action suggested earlier, *in Muzammil* (73) *and Mudaththir* (74).** *This involved some hardship. When the Prophet followed the Divine suggestion, it worked very well.*

C. **[*Āyah* 7 & *āyah* 8]** Contain Suggestion for future action:

They repeat: in the future, also, follow the same policy of action.

When you are relieved from your engagements with the people, devote yourself to the remembrance (*dhikr*) of God.

94 (d) Sūrah Ash-Sharḥ
Understanding and Interpretation

Sūrah Ash-Sharḥ discusses 'how the Prophetic job will become easy?'

God has helped the Prophet in his three basic concerns, which are very similar to those of Moses in 20:25-35:

1. When Moses made *du'ā* (prayer) that God opens his chest, he was looking for conceptual clarity concerning the message he had to deliver so that he understands clearly what needs to be done and how it will be done.
2. He also prayed that the huge burden of his work becomes easy for him.
3. At the end Moses mentioned his ultimate objective: 'So that we both glorify You and make lot of your remembrance (*dhikr*).'
   He meant, 'The remembrance of God, which he and his brother were making, becomes prevalent, i.e., *their mission is triumphant.*

The *sūrah* reaffirms the policy, which was suggested earlier, in *Sūrah al-Muzzammmil* (73) and *Sūrah al-Muddaththir* (74). It is composed of **hardship on two planes**: 'When you finish one kind of hardship (the one related with your missionary work, i.e., doing of your duty as a prophet of God in dealing with various individuals or groups of people etc.), you start another hardship, (i.e., making *ṣalāh,* reciting the Qur'an, doing *dhikr* or remembrance of God'). This policy of action is given the name '*al-'Usr*'or 'the Hardship.' It has worked very successfully and made his job easy. Therefore, the *sūrah* suggests that the Prophet should continue following the same policy of action.

Chapter Fourteen

95 (a) Sūrah at-Tīn

سُوْرَةُ التِّيْنِ

بِسْمِ اللّٰهِ الرَّحْمٰنِ الرَّحِيْمِ

وَالتِّيْنِ وَالزَّيْتُوْنِ ۙ﴿١﴾ وَطُوْرِ سِيْنِيْنَ ۙ﴿٢﴾ وَهٰذَا الْبَلَدِ الْاَمِيْنِ ۙ﴿٣﴾ لَقَدْ
خَلَقْنَا الْاِنْسَانَ فِيْٓ اَحْسَنِ تَقْوِيْمٍ ﴿٤﴾ ثُمَّ رَدَدْنٰهُ اَسْفَلَ سٰفِلِيْنَ ۙ﴿٥﴾
اِلَّا الَّذِيْنَ اٰمَنُوْا وَعَمِلُوا الصّٰلِحٰتِ فَلَهُمْ اَجْرٌ غَيْرُ مَمْنُوْنٍ ؕ﴿٦﴾ فَمَا
يُكَذِّبُكَ بَعْدُ بِالدِّيْنِ ؕ﴿٧﴾ اَلَيْسَ اللّٰهُ بِاَحْكَمِ الْحٰكِمِيْنَ ﴿٨﴾

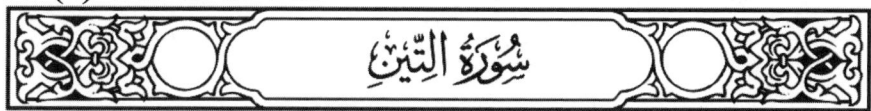

95 (b) Word by word translation of Sūrah at-Tīn

وَالتِّيْنِ وَالزَّيْتُوْنِ ۝١

الزَّيْتُوْنِ	وَ	التِّيْنِ	وَ
the Olive	and	the Fig	By

1. By the Fig and the Olive,

وَطُوْرِ سِيْنِيْنَ ۝٢

سِيْنِيْنَ	طُوْرِ	وَ
Sinai	Mount	By

2. By Mount Sinai,

وَهٰذَا الْبَلَدِ الْاَمِيْنِ ۝٣

الْاَمِيْنِ	الْبَلَدِ	هٰذَا	وَ
The Secure	City	this	By

3. By this Secure City,

لَقَدْ خَلَقْنَا الْاِنْسَانَ فِيْٓ اَحْسَنِ تَقْوِيْمٍ ۝٤

تَقْوِيْمٍ	اَحْسَنِ	فِيْٓ	الْاِنْسَانَ	نَا	خَلَقْ	لَقَدْ
(of) forms	best	In	human being	We	created	Surely

4. Surely, We created human being in the best of forms (i.e., with the best nature).

ثُمَّ رَدَدْنٰهُ اَسْفَلَ سٰفِلِيْنَ ۝٥

سٰفِلِيْنَ	اَسْفَلَ	هُ	رَدَدْنَا	ثُمَّ
of low	to the lowest	him	We degraded	Then

5. Then We degraded him down to the lowest of the low.

اِلَّا الَّذِيْنَ اٰمَنُوْا وَعَمِلُوا الصّٰلِحٰتِ فَلَهُمْ اَجْرٌ غَيْرُ مَمْنُوْنٍ ۝٦

مَمْنُوْنٍ	غَيْرُ	اَجْرٌ	لَهُمْ	فَ	الصّٰلِحٰتِ	وَعَمِلُوا	اٰمَنُوْا	الَّذِيْنَ	اِلَّا
unending	(no)	reward	for them	so is	virtuous deeds	and did	believed	those who	But

6. But those who believed and did virtuous deeds,
so for them is reward unending!

فَمَا يُكَذِّبُكَ بَعْدُ بِالدِّيْنِ ۝٧

الدِّيْنِ	بِ	بَعْدُ	كَ	يُكَذِّبُ	مَا	فَ

<table>
<tr><td>The Religion</td><td>concerning</td><td>after words</td><td>to you</td><td>give a lie</td><td>What</td><td>So</td></tr>
<tr><td colspan="7">7. So, after all this (clarification) concerning ad-Dīn, what is the justification for (someone to say) that you are lying?</td></tr>
</table>

<table>
<tr><td colspan="6">أَلَيْسَ اللّٰهُ بِأَحْكَمِ الْحٰكِمِيْنَ ﴿٨﴾</td></tr>
<tr><td>الْحٰكِمِيْنَ</td><td>أَحْكَمِ</td><td>بِ</td><td>اللّٰهُ</td><td>لَيْسَ</td><td>أَ</td></tr>
<tr><td>of all judges</td><td>The most just</td><td>(with)</td><td>God</td><td>not</td><td>Is</td></tr>
<tr><td colspan="6">8. Is God not The Most Just of all the judges?</td></tr>
</table>

95 (c) Outline Structure of Sūrah at-Tīn

The *sūrah* makes its point in three stages:

A. [*Āyāt* 1-3] present history of the prophetic movement

as evidence for the central theme of the *sūrah*.

B. [*Āyāt* 4-6] develop the central theme in three steps:

Āyah 4 indicates that the three prophetic movements confirm the presence of a potential in human nature for the most excellent moral and spiritual qualities. After all, the prophets were humans.

Āyah 5 describes the extreme degeneration of the people who violently opposed these prophetic missions.

Āyah 6 states that, in the same spiritually degenerated society, there were people who supported the prophets, who believed and did virtuous actions. They shall have unfailing reward from their Lord!

C. [*Āyah* 7 & *āyah* 8] together testify the Religion.

This being the human reality, God, Who is The Most Just of all the Judges, will surely have a Judgment Day.

The Religion is true.

95 (d) Sūrah at-Tīn

Understanding and Interpretation

The *sūrah* makes its point in the light of its reference to the history of the prophetic movements – mainly those led by Jesus, Moses, and Abraham. The message of these prophets, the way they conducted their mission and the excellent character manifested by each of them, is a witness to the good nature of human being. At the same time the rotten society in which they worked and the way their corrupt and unjust opponents responded to these prophets is also a witness to how far human being can go in its state of degeneration. However, the conduct of the virtuous (*ṣālīḥ*) believers who, in spite of this violent opposition (*takdhīb)*, firmly stood with the prophets of God, is fully appreciated by The Merciful God. They will receive a never-ending reward from their Lord in Paradise.

The *sūrah* concludes: The above clearly shows that a Day of Reward and Punishment must come. And what the Religion says is true.

[According to us, the meaning of 95:7 is the following:The Prophet has been proclaiming "There shall be a day when people will receive the reward or punishment for their deeds!" After listening to the argument of 95: 1-6, do these people still say 'it is a lie!' Do they not see that God is the Most Just of all the judges?]

Chapter Fifteen

96 (a) Sūrah al-‘Alaq

سُوْرَةُ الْعَلَقِ

بِسْمِ اللّٰهِ الرَّحْمٰنِ الرَّحِيْمِ

اِقْرَاْ بِاسْمِ رَبِّكَ الَّذِيْ خَلَقَ ﴿١﴾ خَلَقَ الْاِنْسَانَ مِنْ عَلَقٍ ﴿٢﴾ اِقْرَاْ وَرَبُّكَ
الْاَكْرَمُ ﴿٣﴾ الَّذِيْ عَلَّمَ بِالْقَلَمِ ﴿٤﴾ عَلَّمَ الْاِنْسَانَ مَا لَمْ يَعْلَمْ ﴿٥﴾ كَلَّآ اِنَّ
الْاِنْسَانَ لَيَطْغٰۤى ﴿٦﴾ اَنْ رَّاٰهُ اسْتَغْنٰى ﴿٧﴾ اِنَّ اِلٰى رَبِّكَ الرُّجْعٰى ﴿٨﴾ اَرَءَيْتَ
الَّذِيْ يَنْهٰى ﴿٩﴾ عَبْدًا اِذَا صَلّٰى ﴿١٠﴾ اَرَءَيْتَ اِنْ كَانَ عَلَى الْهُدٰۤى ﴿١١﴾ اَوْ اَمَرَ
بِالتَّقْوٰى ﴿١٢﴾ اَرَءَيْتَ اِنْ كَذَّبَ وَتَوَلّٰى ﴿١٣﴾ اَلَمْ يَعْلَمْ بِاَنَّ اللّٰهَ يَرٰى ﴿١٤﴾ كَلَّا
لَئِنْ لَّمْ يَنْتَهِ لَنَسْفَعًا بِالنَّاصِيَةِ ﴿١٥﴾ نَاصِيَةٍ كَاذِبَةٍ خَاطِئَةٍ ﴿١٦﴾ فَلْيَدْعُ
نَادِيَهٗ ﴿١٧﴾ سَنَدْعُ الزَّبَانِيَةَ ﴿١٨﴾ كَلَّا لَا تُطِعْهُ وَاسْجُدْ وَاقْتَرِبْ ﴿١٩﴾

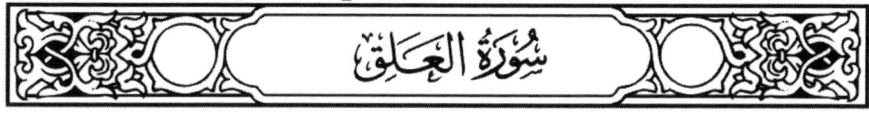

96 (b) Word by word translation of Sūrah al-'Alaq

اِقْرَاْ بِاسْمِ رَبِّكَ الَّذِيْ خَلَقَ ﴿١﴾

خَلَقَ	الَّذِيْ	كَ	رَبِّ	اسْمِ	بِ	اِقْرَاْ
Created	Who	(of) your	Lord	the name	with	Read

1. Read with the name of your Lord Who created.

خَلَقَ الْاِنْسَانَ مِنْ عَلَقٍ ﴿٢﴾

عَلَقٍ	مِنْ	الْاِنْسَانَ	خَلَقَ
a clot	from	human being	(He) created

2. Created human being from a clot.

اِقْرَاْ وَرَبُّكَ الْاَكْرَمُ ﴿٣﴾

الْاَكْرَمُ	كَ	رَبُّ	وَ	اِقْرَاْ
(is) The Most Generous	Your	Lord	and	Read

3. Read and your Lord is the Most Generous,

الَّذِيْ عَلَّمَ بِالْقَلَمِ ﴿٤﴾

الْقَلَمِ	بِ	عَلَّمَ	الَّذِيْ
the pen	with	taught	Who

4. Who taught with the pen.

عَلَّمَ الْاِنْسَانَ مَا لَمْ يَعْلَمْ ﴿٥﴾

يَعْلَمْ	لَمْ	مَا	الْاِنْسَانَ	عَلَّمَ
Know	(he) did not	what	human being	(God)Taught

5. Taught human being what he did not know.

كَلَّآ اِنَّ الْاِنْسَانَ لَيَطْغٰىٓ ﴿٦﴾

يَطْغٰىٓ	لَ	الْاِنْسَانَ	اِنَّ	كَلَّآ
is transgressing	surely	human being	verily	Nay

6. Nay, verily human being is (for sure) in transgression;

اَنْ رَّاٰهُ اسْتَغْنٰى ﴿٧﴾

اسْتَغْنٰى	هُ	رَّاٰ	اَنْ
indepdent / has no need	himself	(he) sees	That

7. That he finds himself independent. (well-off/having no need)

اِنَّ اِلٰى رَبِّكَ الرُّجْعٰى ﴿۸﴾

الرُّجْعٰى	كَ	رَبِّ	اِلٰى	اِنَّ
(is) the return	your	Lord	toward	Verily

8. Verily, toward your Lord is the return!

اَرَءَيْتَ الَّذِيْ يَنْهٰى ﴿۹﴾

يَنْهٰى	الَّذِيْ	رَءَيْتَ	اَ
Forbids	(the person) who	you see	Did

9. Did you see the person who forbids

عَبْدًا اِذَا صَلّٰى ﴿۱۰﴾

صَلّٰى	اِذَا	عَبْدًا
he prays	when	A servant

10. A servant when he prays (offers his *ṣalāh*)

اَرَءَيْتَ اِنْ كَانَ عَلَى الْهُدٰٓى ﴿۱۱﴾

الْهُدٰٓى	عَلَى	كَانَ	اِنْ	رَءَيْتَ	اَ
the guidance	on	he was	if	you see	Did

11. Did you see (think) if (maybe) he were guided,

اَوْ اَمَرَ بِالتَّقْوٰى ﴿۱۲﴾

التَّقْوٰى	بِ	اَمَرَ	اَوْ
piety	(with)	(if) he enjoins	Or

12. Or if he enjoins piety,

اَرَءَيْتَ اِنْ كَذَّبَ وَتَوَلّٰى ﴿۱۳﴾

تَوَلّٰى	وَ	كَذَّبَ	اِنْ	رَءَيْتَ	اَ
turned away	and	he gaves lies	if	you see	Did

13. Did you see, if in spite of it. he gives lies and turns away;

اَلَمْ يَعْلَمْ بِاَنَّ اللّٰهَ يَرٰى ﴿۱۴﴾

يَرٰى	اللّٰهَ	اَنَّ	بِ	يَعْلَمْ	لَمْ	اَ
sees	God	(verily)	(that)	he know	not	Did

14. Did he not know that God sees?

كَلَّا لَئِن لَّمْ يَنتَهِ لَنَسْفَعًا بِالنَّاصِيَةِ ﴿١٥﴾

النَّاصِيَة	بِ	نَسْفَعًا	لَ	يَنتَهِ	لَّمْ	ان	لَ	كَلَّا
(his) forelock	by	We shall drag	surely	he does stop	not	if	(surely)	Nay

15. Nay, if he does not stop, We shall surely drag him by his forelock!

نَاصِيَةٍ كَاذِبَةٍ خَاطِئَةٍ ﴿١٦﴾

خَاطِئَةٍ	كَاذِبَةٍ	نَاصِيَةٍ
criminal	(that is) a liar	Forlock

16. Forelock, which is a liar, criminal!

فَلْيَدْعُ نَادِيَهُ ﴿١٧﴾

هُ	نَادِيَ	يَدْعُ	لْ	فَ
his	henchmen	him call	let	So

17. So let him call his henchmen.

سَنَدْعُ الزَّبَانِيَةَ ﴿١٨﴾

الزَّبَانِيَةَ	نَدْعُ	سَ
the Angels of Hell	We shall call	(Soon)

18. We shall also call the angels of Hell.

كَلَّا لَا تُطِعْهُ وَاسْجُدْ وَاقْتَرِب ﴿١٩﴾

اقْتَرِب	وَ	اسْجُدْ	وَ	هُ	تُطِعْ	لَا	كَلَّا
draw near	and	prostrate yourself	and	him	obey	(do)not	Nay

19. Nay, obey him not, and prostrate yourself and draw near (to God).

96 (c) Outline Structure of Sūrah al-'Alaq

The *sūrah* makes its point in five stages:

A. **[*Āyāt* 1-5] Read (the Book) in the name of your Lord**
Who created human being from a clot,
(Here is the written) Guidance from God, The Most Generous,
Who taught human beings to (read and) write.
Read: what human beings could not have learned without Revelation.

B. **[Āyāt 6-8] The human situation in which reading takes place:**
Transgression in the human world:
No sense of accountability to God, to whom is the return!
Those who are well off, acting arrogantly.

C. **[Āyāt 9-14]** (Reading of the Book creates a Reaction.)
Divine Review: invitation to thinking.
Did you see this criminal act!
(Someone) will not let a servant of God make his prayer.
Will he stand in his way even if he is on the right path?
Even if he is calling the people to piety and virtue?
If he turns away and give lie, in spite of this . . .
Does he not know that God is watching?

D. **[Āyāt 15-18] Warning to the transgressor,**
(to embolden the Reader)
Beware! If he does not stop, I will take action against him
and then no one will be able to help!.

E. **[Āyah 19] To the reader: By way of encouragement.**
Do not submit to any pressure!
(The reading aims at bringing the servant nearer to his Lord.)
'Prostrate and get closer to God.'

96 (d) Sūrah al-'Alaq

Understanding and Interpretation

The previous *sūrah* introduced the prophetic missions of Abraham, Moses and Jesus. Now *Sūrah al-'alaq* initiates a Qur'anic Movement. It is calling the Prophet to 'read' the Book, which will be sent down through installments over twenty three years.

The reading takes place in the context of well-to-do people, acting as transgressors. They are reminded of their return to God for their accountability.

As the Qur'anic Movement proceeds further, readers of the Book – the Prophet and other believers — submit to their Lord, offer their prayer, get more and more involved in the doing of their own duties that follow from their readings. They also remind others of their duties. There is violence against the Reader to stop him from offering his *ṣalāh* (prayer). The Book uses it as an opportunity to awaken the public conscience.

In the warning to the criminals, the purpose is to embolden the readers. God will take care of the criminals; you should not worry at all.

'Do not submit to any pressure; prostrate to get closer to your Lord.'

Chapter Sixteen

97 (d) Sūrah al-Qadr

سُورَةُ الْقَدْرِ

بِسْمِ اللّٰهِ الرَّحْمٰنِ الرَّحِيْمِ

إِنَّآ أَنْزَلْنٰهُ فِي لَيْلَةِ الْقَدْرِ ۝١ وَمَآ أَدْرٰىكَ مَا لَيْلَةُ الْقَدْرِ ۝٢

لَيْلَةُ الْقَدْرِ خَيْرٌ مِّنْ أَلْفِ شَهْرٍ ۝٣ تَنَزَّلُ الْمَلٰٓئِكَةُ وَالرُّوحُ فِيْهَا

بِإِذْنِ رَبِّهِمْ مِّنْ كُلِّ أَمْرٍ ۝٤ سَلٰمٌ هِيَ حَتّٰى مَطْلَعِ الْفَجْرِ ۝٥

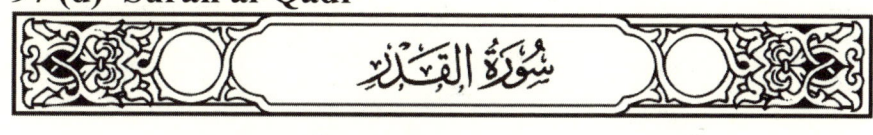

97 (b) Word by word translation of Sūrah al-Qadr

اِنَّآ اَنْزَلْنٰهُ فِيْ لَيْلَةِ الْقَدْرِ ①

الْقَدْرِ	لَيْلَةِ	فِيْ	هُ	اَنْزَلْنَا	اِنَّآ
(of) *Qadr*	The Night	in	it (Qur'an)	We sent down	Verily (We)

1. Verily, We sent it (The Glorious Qur'an) down on the Night of *Qadr*

وَمَآ اَدْرٰىكَ مَا لَيْلَةُ الْقَدْرِ ②

الْقَدْرِ	لَيْلَةُ	مَا	كَ	اَدْرٰى	مَآ	وَ
(of) *Qadr*	The Night	what (is)	You	will make know	what	And

2. And what will make you understand 'what is the Night of *Qadr*?'

لَيْلَةُ الْقَدْرِ خَيْرٌ مِّنْ اَلْفِ شَهْرٍ ③

شَهْرٍ	اَلْفِ	مِّنْ	خَيْرٌ	الْقَدْرِ	لَيْلَةُ
months	one thousand	than	(is) better	(of) *Qadr*	The Night

3. The Night of Qadr is better than one thousand months!

تَنَزَّلُ الْمَلٰٓئِكَةُ وَالرُّوْحُ فِيْهَا بِاِذْنِ رَبِّهِمْ مِنْ كُلِّ اَمْرٍ ④

اَمْرٍ	كُلِّ	مِنْ	رَبِّهِمْ	بِاِذْنِ	فِيْهَا	وَالرُّوْحُ	الْمَلٰٓئِكَةُ	تَنَزَّلُ
Command	each	(with)	(of) their Lord	with permission	(is) in it	and the Spirit	the angels	Decend

4. The angels descend in it, and the Spirit (Gabriel) is (also) amongst them, with the sanction of their Lord, bringing all kinds of (blessed) commands (e.g., decrees for the betterment of human life on earth).

سَلٰمٌ هِيَ حَتّٰى مَطْلَعِ الْفَجْرِ ⑤

الْفَجْرِ	مَطْلَعِ	حَتّٰى	هِيَ	سَلٰمٌ
(of) the dawn	the rise	until	(in) it	Peace (is)

5. Peace is in it until the rise of dawn

97 (c) Outline Structure of Sūrah al-Qadr

The *sūrah* makes its point in four stages:

A. **[*Āyah* 1]** introduces the subject:
The Night of *Qadr* acquired great value,
due to the **sending down of the Qur'an** in this night.

B. **[*Āyah* 2 & Āyah 3]** further underline the importance, in the lunar calendar, of this recurrent event.

C. **[*Āyah* 4] The central *āyah* explains what is actually involved in its being *a very blessed night.***

D. **[*Āyah* 5] This night is peace (from God) from dusk to dawn.**

The concluding *āyah* is, implicitly, reminding the believers that they should not deprive themselves from the blessings of this night. Remember God, as much as possible, by making the best use of the whole night.

97 (d) Sūrah al-Qadr
Understanding and Interpretation

The sending down of the Book is a most blessed occurrence in human history. It takes place at a special point of time in ***Divine Planning***. The Night of *Qadr* or the night when the sending down of the Book took place, is specially marked in the Divine Calendar. The Night of *Qadr* is *celebrated every lunar year* under Divine Sanction as an important festival. The angels of God, under the leadership of Gabriel, descend to the human world – with all kinds blessed commands to the human world.

The peace and blessings of this night continue from dusk to dawn. The believers should not deprive themselves of these benefits. They should remember God more and more, recite the Qur'an, offer *ṣalāh* and ponder over Divine *āyāt.*

Chapter Seventeen

98 (a) Sūrah al-Bayyinah

سُوْرَةُ الْبَيِّنَةِ

بِسْمِ اللّٰهِ الرَّحْمٰنِ الرَّحِيْمِ

لَمْ يَكُنِ الَّذِيْنَ كَفَرُوْا مِنْ اَهْلِ الْكِتٰبِ وَ الْمُشْرِكِيْنَ مُنْفَكِّيْنَ

حَتّٰى تَاْتِيَهُمُ الْبَيِّنَةُ ۙ(١) رَسُوْلٌ مِّنَ اللّٰهِ يَتْلُوْا صُحُفًا مُّطَهَّرَةً ۙ(٢) فِيْهَا

كُتُبٌ قَيِّمَةٌ ؕ(٣) وَ مَا تَفَرَّقَ الَّذِيْنَ اُوْتُوا الْكِتٰبَ اِلَّا مِنْۢ بَعْدِ مَا

جَآءَتْهُمُ الْبَيِّنَةُ ؕ(٤) وَ مَاۤ اُمِرُوْۤا اِلَّا لِيَعْبُدُوا اللّٰهَ مُخْلِصِيْنَ

لَهُ الدِّيْنَ ۙ۬ حُنَفَآءَ وَ يُقِيْمُوا الصَّلٰوةَ وَ يُؤْتُوا الزَّكٰوةَ وَ ذٰلِكَ دِيْنُ

الْقَيِّمَةِ ؕ(٥) اِنَّ الَّذِيْنَ كَفَرُوْا مِنْ اَهْلِ الْكِتٰبِ وَ الْمُشْرِكِيْنَ فِيْ نَارِ

جَهَنَّمَ خٰلِدِيْنَ فِيْهَا ؕ اُولٰٓئِكَ هُمْ شَرُّ الْبَرِيَّةِ ؕ(٦) اِنَّ الَّذِيْنَ اٰمَنُوْا وَ

عَمِلُوا الصّٰلِحٰتِ ۙ اُولٰٓئِكَ هُمْ خَيْرُ الْبَرِيَّةِ ؕ(٧) جَزَآؤُهُمْ عِنْدَ رَبِّهِمْ

جَنّٰتُ عَدْنٍ تَجْرِيْ مِنْ تَحْتِهَا الْاَنْهٰرُ خٰلِدِيْنَ فِيْهَاۤ اَبَدًا ؕ رَضِيَ

اللّٰهُ عَنْهُمْ وَ رَضُوْا عَنْهُ ؕ ذٰلِكَ لِمَنْ خَشِيَ رَبَّهٗ (٨)

98 (b) Word by word translation of Sūrah al-Bayyinah

لَمْ يَكُنِ الَّذِيْنَ كَفَرُوْا مِنْ اَهْلِ الْكِتٰبِ

الْكِتٰبِ	اَهْلِ	مِنْ	كَفَرُوْا	الَّذِيْنَ	يَكُنِ	لَمْ
(of) the Book	The People	from	disblieved	Those who	were	Not

1. (Before the coming of the Qur'an and the Prophet, the condition of) the People of the Book

وَالْمُشْرِكِيْنَ مُنْفَكِّيْنَ حَتّٰى تَاْتِيَهُمُ الْبَيِّنَةُ ۝١

الْبَيِّنَةُ	هُمُ	تَاْتِيَ	حَتّٰى	مُنْفَكِّيْنَ	الْمُشْرِكِيْنَ	وَ
the clear evidence	to them	comes	Until	going to leaeve off	the Pagans	And

.and the Pagans (was such that they) were not going to leave off (their wrong ways) unless the Clear Evidence comes to them.

رَسُوْلٌ مِّنَ اللّٰهِ يَتْلُوْا صُحُفًا مُّطَهَّرَةً ۝٢

مُّطَهَّرَةً	صُحُفًا	يَتْلُوْا	اللّٰهِ	مِّنَ	رَسُوْلٌ
purified	Scriptures	who recites	God	from	A messenger

2. A messenger of God who recites purified scriptures (i.e., *sūrahs*).

فِيْهَا كُتُبٌ قَيِّمَةٌ ۝٣

قَيِّمَةٌ	كُتُبٌ	هَا	فِيْ
with straight teachings	books (ordinances)	it	In

3. Having straight ordinances.

وَمَا تَفَرَّقَ الَّذِيْنَ اُوْتُوا الْكِتٰبَ

الْكِتٰبَ	اُوْتُوا	الَّذِيْنَ	تَفَرَّقَ	مَا	وَ
the Book	were given	those who	became divided	not	And

4. Nor were the People of the Book divided until clear evidence (clear teaching of Torah) came to them!

إِلَّا مِنۢ بَعۡدِ مَا جَآءَتۡهُمُ ٱلۡبَيِّنَةُ ٤

ٱلۡبَيِّنَةُ	هُمُ	جَآءَتۡ	مَا	بَعۡدِ	مِنۢ	إِلَّا
the Clear Evidence	them	came (to)	what	after	(sometime)	But

4. …(That is, this division had occurred only after the coming of the clear evidence in Torah.)

وَمَآ أُمِرُوٓاْ إِلَّا لِيَعۡبُدُواْ ٱللَّهَ مُخۡلِصِينَ لَهُ ٱلدِّينَ

ٱلدِّينَ	لَهُ	مُخۡلِصِينَ	ٱللَّهَ	لِيَعۡبُدُواْ	إِلَّا	أُمِرُوٓاْ	مَآ	وَ
the Religion	to Him	purifying	God	they should worship	but only that	they were commanded	not	And

5. They were commanded only to serve (One) God, being sincere to God in their religion, becoming (men) of pure faith (not mixing up loyalties) and

حُنَفَآءَ وَيُقِيمُواْ ٱلصَّلَوٰةَ وَيُؤۡتُواْ ٱلزَّكَوٰةَۚ وَذَٰلِكَ دِينُ ٱلۡقَيِّمَةِ ٥

ٱلۡقَيِّمَةِ	دِينُ	ذَٰلِكَ	ٱلزَّكَوٰةَ	وَيُؤۡتُواْ	ٱلصَّلَوٰةَ	وَيُقِيمُواْ	حُنَفَآءَ
of The Straight	Religion	that (is)	the charity	and pay	the prayer	and establish	With undivied loyalty

to establish ṣalāh (the prayer) and pay *zakāh* (the charity) and that is the Straight Religion. (That is the religion of the straight nature of human beings, which has no crookedness.)

إِنَّ ٱلَّذِينَ كَفَرُواْ مِنۡ أَهۡلِ ٱلۡكِتَٰبِ وَٱلۡمُشۡرِكِينَ

ٱلۡمُشۡرِكِينَ	وَ	ٱلۡكِتَٰبِ	أَهۡلِ	مِنۡ	كَفَرُواْ	ٱلَّذِينَ	إِنَّ
the Pagans	and	(of) the Book	The People	Fro m	disblieved	those who	Verily

6. Verily, those who disbelieved from the People of the Book and the Pagans

فِي نَارِ جَهَنَّمَ خَٰلِدِينَ فِيهَآۚ أُوْلَٰٓئِكَ هُمۡ شَرُّ ٱلۡبَرِيَّةِ ٦

ٱلۡبَرِيَّةِ	شَرُّ	هُمۡ	أُوْلَٰٓئِكَ	فِيهَآ	خَٰلِدِينَ	جَهَنَّمَ	نَارِ	فِي
(of) the creatures	the worst	they (are)	those	in it	(will) abide	Hell	Fire	(are) in

are in the Hellfire, therein dwelling forever, and those are the worst of the creatures.

اِنَّ الَّذِيْنَ اٰمَنُوْا وَعَمِلُوا الصّٰلِحٰتِ اُولٰٓئِكَ هُمْ خَيْرُ الْبَرِيَّةِ ۝٧

الْبَرِيَّةِ ؕ	خَيْرُ	هُمْ	اُولٰٓئِكَ	الصّٰلِحٰتِ	وَعَمِلُوا	اٰمَنُوْا	الَّذِيْنَ	اِنَّ
(of) the creatures	the best	they (are)	those	virtuous deeds	and did	believed	those who	Verily

7. Verily, they who believed and did virtuous deeds, those are the best of the creatures.

جَزَآؤُهُمْ عِنْدَ رَبِّهِمْ جَنّٰتُ عَدْنٍ تَجْرِيْ مِنْ تَحْتِهَا

تَحْتِهَا	مِنْ	تَجْرِيْ	عَدْنٍ	جَنّٰتُ	رَبِّهِمْ	عِنْدَ	هُمْ	جَزَآؤُ
under which	(from)	flow	evergreen	Gardens	their Lord	(near)	their	reward (is)

8. Their reward is with their Lord, evergreen Gardens under

الْاَنْهٰرُ خٰلِدِيْنَ فِيْهَآ اَبَدًا ؕ رَضِيَ اللّٰهُ عَنْهُمْ

هُمْ	عَنْ	اللّٰهُ	رَضِيَ	اَبَدًا	هَآ	فِيْ	خٰلِدِيْنَ	الْاَنْهٰرُ
them	with	God	(is) pleased	forever	It	In	they will abide	the rivers

which rivers flow, dwelling therein for ever and ever. God is well-pleased with them.

وَرَضُوْا عَنْهُ ذٰلِكَ لِمَنْ خَشِيَ رَبَّهٗ ۝٨

هٗ	رَبَّ	خَشِيَ	مَنْ	لِ	ذٰلِكَ	عَنْهُ	رَضُوْا	وَ
his	Lord	fears	one who	for	that is	with Him	they are pleased	and

and they are well-pleased (with their Lord). That is for one, who fears his/her Lord.

98 (c) Outline Structure of Sūrah al-Bayyinah

The *sūrah* makes its point in four stages:

A. [*Āyāt* 1-3] The present *disbelief* of the People of the Book and the Pagans is totally un-justified. It is quite evident to every honest person that *here is a prophet of God, reciting Divine scriptures!*

B. [*Āyāt* 4-5] Earlier *division* of the People of the Book was as unjustified as their *present disbelief.* Both Torah as well as the Qur'an invite the people to become one family of the servants of One God alone - in belief and action.

C. [*Āyah* 6] Therefore, worst of all creatures are disbelievers – both from the People of the Book and from the Pagans.

They will be in Hellfire!

D. [*Āyah* 7 & *Āyah* 8] Believers who did virtuous actions are the best of creatures. They will be honored in the Vicinity of their Lord, living forever in the evergreen, everlasting Gardens. God is pleased with them and they are pleased with God.

98 (d) Sūrah al-Bayyinah
Understanding and Interpretation

The *sūrah* makes it clear that the disbelief of the People of the Book as well as that of The Pagans of Makkah is not due to an innocent ignorance. All that was required to make it clear to them 'that the Qur'an is a Divine Revelation and that the Prophet is a true prophet of God' has been done in a perfect manner.

The *sūrah* makes it clear that earlier also the ***tawḥīdic*** **message – its theory as well as practice – was made quite clear** to the People of the Book, but they left its central message and became divided into various sects.

The *Sūrah al-Bayyinah* (98) proclaims that those who, due to their vested interests, knowingly rejected the Divine invitation to join this community of believers are the worst of God's creatures and shall reside in Hellfire permanantly.

On the other hand those who believed and did virtuous actions in spite of the difficult situation created by these opponents are the best of the creatures. God will enter them into everlasting evergreen Gardens. They are pleased with their Lord and their Lord is pleased with them, here as well as in the Herafter.

Chapter Eighteen

99 (a) Sūrah az-Zalzalah

سُورَةُ الزَّلْزَلَةِ

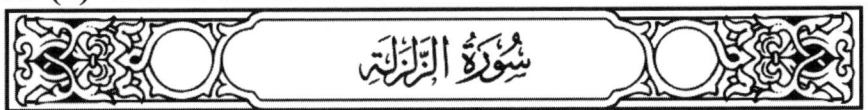

بِسْمِ اللّٰهِ الرَّحْمٰنِ الرَّحِيْمِ

إِذَا زُلْزِلَتِ الْأَرْضُ زِلْزَالَهَا ﴿١﴾ وَأَخْرَجَتِ الْأَرْضُ أَثْقَالَهَا ﴿٢﴾ وَقَالَ
الْإِنْسَانُ مَا لَهَا ﴿٣﴾ يَوْمَئِذٍ تُحَدِّثُ أَخْبَارَهَا ﴿٤﴾ بِأَنَّ رَبَّكَ أَوْحٰى لَهَا ﴿٥﴾
يَوْمَئِذٍ يَّصْدُرُ النَّاسُ أَشْتَاتًا لِّيُرَوْا أَعْمَالَهُمْ ﴿٦﴾ فَمَنْ يَّعْمَلْ مِثْقَالَ
ذَرَّةٍ خَيْرًا يَّرَهُ ﴿٧﴾ وَمَنْ يَّعْمَلْ مِثْقَالَ ذَرَّةٍ شَرًّا يَّرَهُ ﴿٨﴾

99 (b) Word by word translation of Sūrah Az-Zalzalah

اِذَا زُلْزِلَتِ الْاَرْضُ زِلْزَالَهَا ﴿١﴾

هَا	زِلْزَالَ	الْاَرْضُ	زُلْزِلَتِ	اِذَا
(with) its	Quack	the Earth	(is) shaken	When

1. When the Earth is shaken with its (utmost) quake,

وَاَخْرَجَتِ الْاَرْضُ اَثْقَالَهَا ﴿٢﴾

هَا	اَثْقَالَ	الْاَرْضُ	اَخْرَجَتِ	وَ
its	Burdens	the Earth	takes out	And

2. And the earth throws out its burdens (humans buried in it, some of them criminals),

وَقَالَ الْاِنْسَانُ مَا لَهَا ﴿٣﴾

هَا	لَ	مَا	الْاِنْسَانُ	قَالَ	وَ
it	(wrong) with	what (is)	the human	says	And

3. And human being says 'what is (wrong) with it?'.

يَوْمَئِذٍ تُحَدِّثُ اَخْبَارَهَا ﴿٤﴾

هَا	اَخْبَارَ	تُحَدِّثُ	يَوْمَئِذٍ
its	news	it will relate	That day

4. That day, it (Earth) will relate its news (i.e., whatever happened on it).

بِاَنَّ رَبَّكَ اَوْحٰى لَهَا ﴿٥﴾

هَا	اَوْحٰى	كَ	رَبَّ	اَنَّ	بِ
It	will command	your	Lord	(verily)	Because

5. Because your Lord will command it.

يَوْمَئِذٍ يَّصْدُرُ النَّاسُ اَشْتَاتًا لِّيُرَوْا اَعْمَالَهُمْ ﴿٦﴾

هُمْ	اَعْمَالَ	يُرَوْا	لِ	اَشْتَاتًا	النَّاسُ	يَّصْدُرُ	يَوْمَئِذٍ
their	works	to be shown	(in order)	scattered (in group)	the people	will come out	That day

6. That day the people will come out, scattered (in groups), to be shown their works.

فَمَنْ يَّعْمَلْ مِثْقَالَ ذَرَّةٍ خَيْرًا يَّرَهٗ ﴿٧﴾

هٗ	يَّرَ	خَيْرًا	ذَرَّةٍ	مِثْقَالَ	يَّعْمَلْ	مَنْ	فَ

It	(he) will see	(of) good	an atom	weight	does	whoever	So
7. So, whoever does an atom of good, he shall see it.							
وَمَنْ يَّعْمَلْ مِثْقَالَ ذَرَّةٍ شَرًّا يَّرَهٗ ۝٨							
هٗ	يَّرَ	شَرًّا	ذَرَّةٍ	مِثْقَالَ	يَّعْمَلْ	مَنْ	وَ
It	(he) will see	(of) evil	an atom	weight	does	whoever	So
8. And whoever does an atom of evil, he shall see it.							

99 (c) Outline Structure of Sūrah az-Zalzalah

The *sūrah* makes its point in three stages:

A. **[*Āyāt* 1-3] introduce the subject:**

What will happen when the Earth will throw out, through a great quake, the burden (the dead bodies of the criminals) it has been carrying inside its belly, and human beings will wonder what is wrong with the Earth?

(The *sūrah* gives its answer to the above question in two installments.)

B. **[*Āyah* 4 & *āyah* 5] contain the first installment of the answer:** That will be the day when God will command the Earth and it will start relating its story - all that happened in the world through ages.

C. **[*Āyāt* 6-8] contain the second installment:**

That will be the day when scattered groups of people will come out: everyone shall see whatever he or she has done, even if it is an extremely small good or evil action.

99 (d) Sūrah az-Zalzalah
Understanding and Interpretation

Criminal activities which are being committed on earth by various groups of criminals are all being recorded. A day will come when there will be a horrible earthquake, and the earth will throw out the bodies of these criminals – the burden which it would reluctantly keep within its belly till Judgment Day. Scattered groups will gather to see the records of their actions. On that day, God will direct the Earth to tell its story, and it will start relating the details of all that happened on its surface.

Chapter Ninteen

100 (a) Sūrah al-'Ādiyāt

سُورَةُ العَادِيَاتِ

بِسْمِ اللّٰهِ الرَّحْمٰنِ الرَّحِيْمِ

وَالْعٰدِيٰتِ ضَبْحًا ﴿١﴾ فَالْمُوْرِيٰتِ قَدْحًا ﴿٢﴾ فَالْمُغِيْرٰتِ صُبْحًا ﴿٣﴾ فَاَثَرْنَ

بِهٖ نَقْعًا ﴿٤﴾ فَوَسَطْنَ بِهٖ جَمْعًا ﴿٥﴾ اِنَّ الْاِنْسَانَ لِرَبِّهٖ لَكَنُوْدٌ ﴿٦﴾ وَاِنَّهٗ عَلٰى

ذٰلِكَ لَشَهِيْدٌ ﴿٧﴾ وَاِنَّهٗ لِحُبِّ الْخَيْرِ لَشَدِيْدٌ ﴿٨﴾ اَفَلَا يَعْلَمُ اِذَا بُعْثِرَ مَا

فِي الْقُبُوْرِ ﴿٩﴾ وَحُصِّلَ مَا فِي الصُّدُوْرِ ﴿١٠﴾ اِنَّ رَبَّهُمْ بِهِمْ يَوْمَئِذٍ لَّخَبِيْرٌ ﴿١١﴾

100 (b) Word by word translation of Sūrah al-'Ādiyat

وَالْعٰدِيٰتِ ضَبْحًا ۙ (١)

ضَبْحًا	الْعٰدِيٰتِ	وَ
running with panting breath	the snorting chargers	By

1. By the snorting chargers (horses that run with panting breath),

فَالْمُوْرِيٰتِ قَدْحًا ۙ (٢)

قَدْحًا	الْمُوْرِيٰتِ	فَ
(as they) strike off	sparking (with their hoofs)	Then

2. Those who, thereby, strike off sparks (with their hoofs),

فَالْمُغِيْرٰتِ صُبْحًا ۙ (٣)

صُبْحًا	الْمُغِيْرٰتِ	فَ
at dawn	(they are) those who raid	Then

And who raid at dawn,

فَاَثَرْنَ بِهٖ نَقْعًا ۙ (٤)

نَقْعًا	هٖ	بِ	اَثَرْنَ	فَ
cloud of dust	It	with	raising	Then

4. While raising clouds of dust (at dawn),

فَوَسَطْنَ بِهٖ جَمْعًا ۙ (٥)

جَمْعًا	هٖ	بِ	وَسَطْنَ	فَ
(of) troops	it	with	(they) dash into the middle	Thereby

5. Thereby, they dash into the middle of the troops (at dawn).

اِنَّ الْاِنْسَانَ لِرَبِّهٖ لَكَنُوْدٌ ۚ (٦)

كَنُوْدٌ	لَ	هٖ	رَبِّ	لِ	الْاِنْسَانَ	اِنَّ

ungrateful	(surely)	his	Lord	to	human being (is)	Verily

6. Surely, human being is ungrateful to his Lord.

وَاِنَّهٗ عَلٰى ذٰلِكَ لَشَهِيْدٌ ﴿٧﴾

شَهِيْدٌ	لَ	ذٰلِكَ	عَلٰى	هٗ	اِنَّ	وَ
witness	surely	that	Upon	he (is) (himself)	verily	And

7. And surely, he is (himself) a witness to that.

وَاِنَّهٗ لِحُبِّ الْخَيْرِ لَشَدِيْدٌ ﴿٨﴾

شَدِيْدٌ	لَ	الْخَيْرِ	حُبِّ	لِ	هٗ	اِنَّ	وَ
violent	surely	(of) wealth	the love	for	he (is)	verily	And

8. And surely, he is violent in love of wealth.

اَفَلَا يَعْلَمُ اِذَا بُعْثِرَ مَا فِي الْقُبُوْرِ ﴿٩﴾

الْقُبُوْرِ	فِي	مَا	بُعْثِرَ	اِذَا	يَعْلَمُ	لَا	فَ	اَ
the graves	in	what is	tumbled out	when	he know	not	then	Does

9. Then, does he not know a time will come when the graves will be tumbled out.

وَحُصِّلَ مَا فِي الصُّدُوْرِ ﴿١٠﴾

الصُّدُوْرِ	فِي	مَا	حُصِّلَ	وَ
the breasts (is hidden)	In	whatever is	is taken out	And

10. And whatever is hidden in the breasts is taken out (and made available for cross-examination!)

اِنَّ رَبَّهُمْ بِهِمْ يَوْمَئِذٍ لَّخَبِيْرٌ ﴿١١﴾

خَبِيْرٌ	لَ	يَوْمَئِذٍ	هِمْ	بِ	هُمْ	رَبَّ	اِنَّ
well-informed	surely	that day	them	with	their	Lord	Verily

11. Verily, on that Day, their Lord, shall be well-informed of them.

100 (c) Outline Structure of Sūrah al-'Ādiyāt

The *sūrah* makes its point in three stages:

A. **[*Āyāt* 1-5] The swearing introduces a perspective to highlight the point of *sūrah's* main concern:** Human beings should consider the loyalty of their own horses to them and then examine their own ingratitude to their own Master, who takes care of all of their needs.

B. **[*Āyāt* 6-8] Contain the central theme**

Āyah 6: The above perspective makes it clear how severe human beings's ingratitude is.

Āyah 7 human beings himself will witness 'how thankless he is!'

Āyah 8 further clarifies: It is due to human beings's love of wealth and his being lost in the pursuit of immediate gains.

C. **[*Āyāt* 9-11] Concluding *āyāt* raise a serious question:**

Does human beings not know a day will come when the graves will be emptied and human bodies buried in them will be thrown out?

On that day the secret crimes hidden inside the chests will be taken out and made available for trial.

And then adds:

Their Lord does know what is going to be their fate that day!

100 (d) Sūrah al-'Ādiyāt
Understanding and Interpretation

The *sūrah* deals at length with the loyalty of the horses to their masters - mainly those who are used in the battlefield and who raid the enemy's camp at dawn. Human beings should **learn a lesson from their loyaty.**

Human beings's ingratitude is an obvious reality; human beings themselves will witness how thankless they are!

The *sūrah* suggests that the root cause is the love of wealth. Human beings are lost in the pursuit of immediate gains and they neglect the Hereafter.

We are so involved in enjoying Divine blessing that we do not find time for our thanksgiving to our Merciful Lord.

At the end, the *sūrah* raises a serious question: **Do the criminals, who are hiding their crimes, not think of the day when they will come out of their graves and the secrets hidden within their chests will be taken out?**

And then comments: **their Lord knows very well what is going to be their fate on that day!**

Chapter Twenty

101 (a) Sūrah al-Qāri‘ah

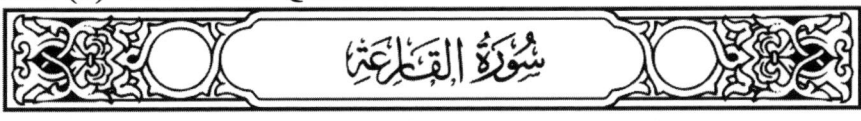

سُورَةُ الْقَارِعَةِ

بِسْمِ ٱللَّهِ ٱلرَّحْمَٰنِ ٱلرَّحِيمِ

ٱلْقَارِعَةُ ﴿١﴾ مَا ٱلْقَارِعَةُ ﴿٢﴾ وَمَآ أَدْرَىٰكَ مَا ٱلْقَارِعَةُ ﴿٣﴾ يَوْمَ يَكُونُ
ٱلنَّاسُ كَٱلْفَرَاشِ ٱلْمَبْثُوثِ ﴿٤﴾ وَتَكُونُ ٱلْجِبَالُ كَٱلْعِهْنِ ٱلْمَنفُوشِ ﴿٥﴾
فَأَمَّا مَن ثَقُلَتْ مَوَٰزِينُهُۥ ﴿٦﴾ فَهُوَ فِى عِيشَةٍ رَّاضِيَةٍ ﴿٧﴾ وَأَمَّا مَنْ خَفَّتْ
مَوَٰزِينُهُۥ ﴿٨﴾ فَأُمُّهُۥ هَاوِيَةٌ ﴿٩﴾ وَمَآ أَدْرَىٰكَ مَا هِيَهْ ﴿١٠﴾ نَارٌ حَامِيَةٌۢ ﴿١١﴾

101(b) Word by word translation of Sūrah al-Qāri'ah

اَلْقَارِعَةُ ۝١ مَا الْقَارِعَةُ ۝٢		
اَلْقَارِعَةُ	مَا	اَلْقَارِعَةُ
The Striking Calamity!	What is	The Striking Calamity!
1. The Striking Calamity! 2. What is the Striking Calamity?		

وَمَآ اَدْرٰىكَ مَا الْقَارِعَةُ ۝٣					
اَلْقَارِعَةُ	مَا	كَ	اَدْرٰ	مَآ	وَ
The Striking Calamity!	what is	you	will make understand	what	And
3. And do you realize: 'what is the Striking Calamity?'					

يَوْمَ يَكُوْنُ النَّاسُ كَالْفَرَاشِ الْمَبْثُوْثِ ۝٤					
الْمَبْثُوْثِ	الْفَرَاشِ	كَ	النَّاسُ	يَكُوْنُ	يَوْمَ
scattered	(the) moths	like	the people	will be	(That) day
4. (Think of) the day when people will be like moths scattered!					

وَتَكُوْنُ الْجِبَالُ كَالْعِهْنِ الْمَنْفُوْشِ ۝٥					
الْمَنْفُوْشِ	الْعِهْنِ	كَ	الْجِبَالُ	تَكُوْنُ	وَ
the carded	wool	like	the mountain	will be	And
5. And when the mountains will be like wool carded.					

فَاَمَّا مَنْ ثَقُلَتْ مَوَازِيْنُهٗ ۝٦					
هٗ	مَوَازِيْنُ	ثَقُلَتْ	مَنْ	اَمَّا	فَ
his	scales	(are) heavy	those whose	as far as	So
6. So far as for him, whose scales are heavy! (whose deeds carry weight!)					

فَهُوَ فِيْ عِيْشَةٍ رَّاضِيَةٍ ۝٧				
رَّاضِيَةٍ	عِيْشَةٍ	فِيْ	هُوَ	فَ
well-pleased with	a life	in	he will be	Then
7. He shall be in a life well-pleased with!				

وَاَمَّا مَنْ خَفَّتْ مَوَازِيْنُهٗ ۝٨					
هٗ	مَوَازِيْنُ	خَفَّتْ	مَنْ	اَمَّا	وَ
his	scales	(are) light	those whose	as for as	And

8. And as for him, whose scales are light! (whose actions carry no weight!)
فَأُمُّهُۥ هَاوِيَةٌ ٩

هَاوِيَةٌ	هُۥ	أُمُّ	فَ
is a pit	his	home (mother)	So

9. His home (mother) will be a pit (an abyss)!
وَمَآ أَدْرَىٰكَ مَا هِيَهْ ١٠ نَارٌ حَامِيَةٌ ١١

حَامِيَةٌ	نَارٌ	هِيَهْ	مَا	كَ	أَدْرٰ	مَآ	وَ
a scorching	fire	this	what (is)	you	make understand	what	And

10. And do you realize: 'what is this (pit)?' 11. It is a scorching fire!

101 (c) Outline Structure of Sūrah al-Qāri'ah

The *sūrah* makes its point in three stages:

A. **[*Āyāt* 1-3] The *sūrah* will talk about a horrible day.**

B. **[*Āyah* 4 & *āyah* 5] explain the nature of that day:**

Objects that seem to have great value or weight today will lose all their value or weight on that day.

The above point is explained:

1. Through the example of humans, some of whom possess great prestige and high position in this life.
2. Through the example of (stony) mountains which are firmly rooted at their places.

C. **[*Āyāt* 6-11] How that Day makes a difference in an individual's destiny.** *Āyāt* (6-7) deal with those individuals whose actions will have weight on that day. *Āyāt* (8-11) deal with those whose actions will be weightless.

101 (d) Sūrah al-Qāri'ah
Understanding and Interpretation

The *sūrah* aims at correcting our perspective. Today wealth and power have importance for us; moral and spiritual considerations do not carry any weight. The Divine concern is that our actions should have weight on the Judgment Day.

The way the state of affairs is, in this temporary phase of life; it is not going to last forever. The *sūrah* starts with some kind of hammering to awaken us. When we *wake up we find ourselves in a very different world***.**

In this life, goodness of action does not seem to posses any value. Politically important people, and the people who possess material resources, have great prestige and honor in human society. On Judgment Day these people will lose all their weight. They will be scattered over the earth like moths.

In the present world, huge stony mountains seem to be permanently fixed at their places. No one can move them. That day these mountains will be mobile like carded wool.

To attain Ultimate Happiness and Success, it is required that our actions carry weight. Those individuals whose actions carry weight will enjoy a happy life, forever. Those whose actions are weightless are doomed. Their permanent residence will be in the Hellfire.

Chapter Twenty One

102 (a) Sūrah at-Takāthur

سُوۡرَةُ التَّكَاثُرِ

بِسۡمِ اللّٰهِ الرَّحۡمٰنِ الرَّحِيۡمِ

أَلۡهٰكُمُ التَّكَاثُرُ ۙ﴿۱﴾ حَتّٰى زُرۡتُمُ الۡمَقَابِرَ ؕ﴿۲﴾ كَلَّا سَوۡفَ تَعۡلَمُوۡنَ ۙ﴿۳﴾ ثُمَّ كَلَّا
سَوۡفَ تَعۡلَمُوۡنَ ؕ﴿۴﴾ كَلَّا لَوۡ تَعۡلَمُوۡنَ عِلۡمَ الۡيَقِيۡنِ ؕ﴿۵﴾ لَتَرَوُنَّ الۡجَحِيۡمَ ۙ﴿۶﴾
ثُمَّ لَتَرَوُنَّهَا عَيۡنَ الۡيَقِيۡنِ ۙ﴿۷﴾ ثُمَّ لَتُسۡـَٔلُنَّ يَوۡمَئِذٍ عَنِ النَّعِيۡمِ ﴿۸﴾

102 (b) Word by word translation of Sūrah At-Takāthur

أَلْهٰكُمُ التَّكَاثُرُ ۝١		
التَّكَاثُرُ	كُمُ	أَلْهٰى
the competition in worldly gains	you	Obsessed
1. You remained obsessed by your mutual competition for more and more worldly gains!		

حَتّٰى زُرْتُمُ الْمَقَابِرَ ۝٢		
الْمَقَابِرَ	زُرْتُمُ	حَتّٰى
the graves	you visited	Until
2. Until you visited the graves.		

كَلَّا سَوْفَ تَعْلَمُوْنَ ۝٣		
تَعْلَمُوْنَ	سَوْفَ	كَلَّا
you will know	soon	By no means
3. By no means! soon you will know.		

ثُمَّ كَلَّا سَوْفَ تَعْلَمُوْنَ ۝٤			
تَعْلَمُوْنَ	سَوْفَ	كَلَّا	ثُمَّ
you will know	soon	by no means	Again
4. Again by no means! soon you will know.			

كَلَّا لَوْ تَعْلَمُوْنَ عِلْمَ الْيَقِيْنِ ۝٥				
الْيَقِيْنِ	عِلْمَ	تَعْلَمُوْنَ	لَوْ	كَلَّا
of surety	(with) the knowledge	you would have known	only if	Nay
5. Nay! If you could but know (it) with sure knowledge!				

لَتَرَوُنَّ الْجَحِيْمَ ۝٦		
الْجَحِيْمَ	تَرَوُنَّ	لَ
the Hell	you will see	Surely
6. Surely, you will see the Hell.		

ثُمَّ لَتَرَوُنَّهَا عَيْنَ الْيَقِيْنِ ۝٧					
الْيَقِيْنِ	عَيْنَ	هَا	تَرَوُنَّ	لَ	ثُمَّ

(of) certainity	with the eye	it	you will see	surely	Then
7. Then, surely, you will see it with the eye of certainty.					
ثُمَّ لَتُسۡـَٔلُنَّ يَوۡمَئِذٍ عَنِ ٱلنَّعِيمِ ﴿٨﴾					
ٱلنَّعِيمِ	عَنِ	يَوۡمَئِذٍ	تُسۡـَٔلُنَّ	لَ	ثُمَّ
the blessings (of God)	about	(on) that day	you will be questioned	surely	Then
8. Then, surely, you will be questioned that day concerning the blessings (of God).					

102 (c) Outline Structure of Sūrah At-Takāthur

The *sūrah* makes its point in three stages:

A. [*Āyah* 1 & *āyah* 2] together introduce the *sūrah*:

Āyah 1: your competing with each other in having more and more worldly gains makes you thanklessly neglect your accountability.
Āyah 2: This forgetfulness will come to an end with one's death.

On reaching the grave, one immediately wakes up from this forgetfulness.

B. [*Āyāt* 3-7] deal with various psychological states, one by one, during one's life journey:

Āyah 3 & *Āyah* 4 (right now) repeatedly hammer to awaken the listeners from their deep slumber.
Āyah 5 deals (implicitly) with the psychological state in which one's negligence is mixed with skepticism. There is, sometimes, an inner voice – giving one a warning. But one rejects it as a whim, saying 'What is the *surety* that there will be a Day of Judgment?'
'It is only a hypothesis.'
Āyah 6 & *āyah* 7: When they see the Hell, they recover from this skepticism.

C. [*Āyah* 8] On that day, you will be questioned:

'God gave you all these blessings; did you do any thanksgiving?'
Thus people's ingratitude is the real issue.

102 (d) Sūrah At-Takāthur
Understanding and Interpretation

The *sūrah* invites its addressees to consider what makes them so forgetful of their duty to God and so ungrateful to their Benefactor. The society of which they are a part is, as a whole, aimlessly running after more and more worldly gains, each of its members competing with each other. There is no sense of gratitude to their Benefactor, no sense of accountability to the Lord of Humankind and thereby little sharing and concern with the downtrodden and alienated sections of society. People are so obsessed by their competition in the pursuit of the worldly benefits that any reminder concerning the Hereafter, for example, by the Quran itself, or by one's own inner voice, is rejected on the ground that it is not one hundred percent sure that there will be a punishment of Hellfire. The *sūrah* comments: you will achieve one hundred percent surety when it will be too late!

Chapter Twenty Two

103 (a) Sūrah al-‘Aṣr

سُورَةُ العَصْرِ

بِسْمِ اللَّهِ الرَّحْمَٰنِ الرَّحِيمِ

وَالْعَصْرِ ﴿١﴾ إِنَّ الْإِنْسَانَ لَفِي خُسْرٍ ﴿٢﴾ إِلَّا الَّذِينَ آمَنُوا وَ
عَمِلُوا الصَّالِحَاتِ وَتَوَاصَوْا بِالْحَقِّ وَتَوَاصَوْا بِالصَّبْرِ ﴿٣﴾

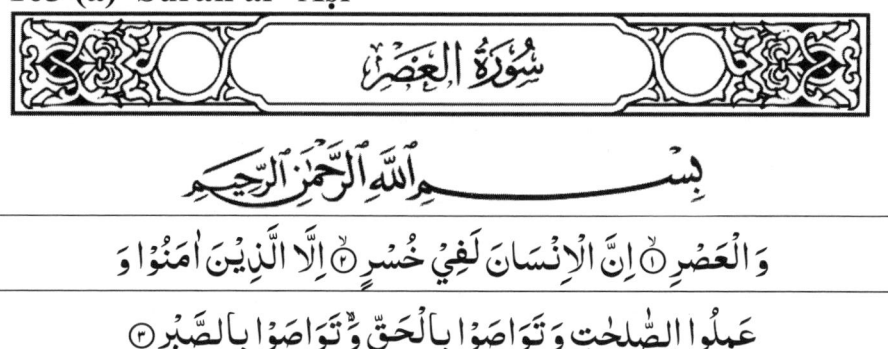

103 (b) Word by word translation of Sūrah al-‘Aṣr

وَالْعَصْرِ ۝١		
عَصْرِ	الْ	وَ
(passing of) time	the	By
1. I swear, by the passage of time,		

اِنَّ الْاِنْسَانَ لَفِيْ خُسْرٍ ۝٢				
خُسْرٍ	فِيْ	لَ	الْاِنْسَانَ	اِنَّ
loss	in	surely	human being (is)	Verily
2. Surely, human being is in loss!				

اِلَّا الَّذِيْنَ اٰمَنُوْا وَعَمِلُوا الصّٰلِحٰتِ					
الصّٰلِحٰتِ	عَمِلُو	وَ	اٰمَنُوْا	الَّذِيْنَ	اِلَّا
virtuous deeds	did	and	believed	those who	But
3. It will be an an altogether different situation, if the people believed and did virtuous deeds,					

وَتَوَاصَوْا بِالْحَقِّ ۙ وَتَوَاصَوْا بِالصَّبْرِ ۝٣							
الصَّبْرِ	بِ	تَوَاصَوْا	وَ	الْحَقِّ	بِ	تَوَاصَوْا	وَ
steadfastness	with	exhorted each other	and	the truth/	with	exhorted each other	and
enjoined upon each other to do their mutual duties and to stand with Truth and enjoined upon each other to be steadfast. (In that case, human beings will achieve *Falāḥ*).							

103 (c) Outline Structure of Sūrah al-'Aṣr

The *sūrah* makes it point in three stages:

A. **[*Āyah* 1] reminds us that *we learn a lesson from the past* history as related in the Qur'an. The time allotted to humankind is running out:** The *qasam* reminds us how Divine Punishment eliminated earlier civilizations which had material progress and technological advancement but they became spiritually and morally bankrupt. They transgressed against God, created corruption, social and economic injustice, and did not correct themselves in spite of the repeated warnings of the prophets of God.

B. **[*Āyah* 2] Present Human Situation**

'Surely, today (also) humankind is rushing toward utter loss *(khusrān)*.'

(The above is the response to the swearing (*jawab qasam)*. The purpose of the *qasam is* to make people serious about this truth.)

C. **[*Āyah* 3] Possibility of a glorious future for humanity!**

Third *āyah* shows the path of *Falāḥ,* i.e., True Happiness or Ultimate Success. It lays down four points.

1. Join the *Tawḥīdic* Movement of the prophets of God that the Prophet, peace be upon him, is leading today.
   (Stop all *shirk* that is causing corruption and exploitation.)
2. Start doing virtuous (*ṣāliḥ*) deeds.
3. Exhort each other to follow the Truth (*ḥaqq*) and do our duties (*ḥuqūq*).
4. Enjoin upon each other to be steadfast and persevering.

103 (d) Sūrah al-'Aṣr
Understanding and Interpretation

The Qur'an is concerned that the purpose of the creation of human beings is fulfilled and human beings achieve *al-Falāḥ* (Ultimate Success & Happiness). To attain this objective, the *sūrah* **starts with a warning, by way of reminding, but ends up with good news which is tied with a clear-cut program of action.** The *sūrah* describes in a nutshell what the Book discusses in full details at various places. The lesson is drawn from the history of earlier human civilizations as reviewed in the Qur'an.

Today again, there is transgression against God. There is corruption everywhere on earth. The message of the prophets of God is totally neglected. **Humanity is (again) heading toward self-destruction.**

However, if the people follow the **four-point program of action, which the *sūrah* recommends,** this situation will change:

Believing is 'coming out of the servitude of other than God and joining the community of believers'. The doing of *ṣālīḥāt* (virtuous actions versus *fāsidāt* or corrupt ones) is just fulfilling the practical implications of our *īmān* (belief).

Believing and doing virtuous actions is necessary but not sufficient to save humankind. *A movement is to be launched to encourage each other to do our social obligations and to give moral support to each other* when we are tested in our way and when we face difficulties.

It is interesting to note that the major part of the *sūrah* deals with the positive aspect. It systematically deals with *the practical question: How we can attain Ultimate Happiness and Success (al-Falāḥ)?*

Chapter Twenty Three

104 (a) Sūrah al Humazah

سُورَةُ الْهُمَزَةِ

بِسْمِ اللَّهِ الرَّحْمَٰنِ الرَّحِيمِ

وَيْلٌ لِّكُلِّ هُمَزَةٍ لُّمَزَةٍ (١) الَّذِي جَمَعَ مَالًا وَعَدَّدَهُ (٢) يَحْسَبُ أَنَّ
مَالَهُ أَخْلَدَهُ (٣) كَلَّا لَيُنبَذَنَّ فِي الْحُطَمَةِ (٤) وَمَا أَدْرَاكَ مَا
الْحُطَمَةُ (٥) نَارُ اللَّهِ الْمُوقَدَةُ (٦) الَّتِي تَطَّلِعُ عَلَى الْأَفْئِدَةِ (٧)
إِنَّهَا عَلَيْهِم مُّؤْصَدَةٌ (٨) فِي عَمَدٍ مُّمَدَّدَةٍ (٩)

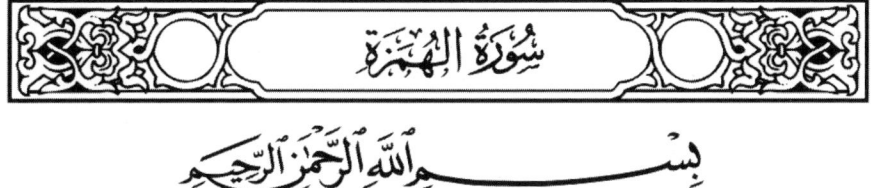

104 (b) Word by word translation of Sūrah al-Humazah

وَيۡلٌ لِّكُلِّ هُمَزَةٍ لُّمَزَةِ ۙ ١

لُّمَزَةٍ	هُمَزَةٍ	كُلِّ	لِّ	وَيۡلٌ
backbiter	slanderer	every	to	Woe

1. Woe to every slanderer, backbiter,

الَّذِيۡ جَمَعَ مَالًا وَّ عَدَّدَهٗ ۙ ٢

عَدَّدَهٗ	وَّ	مَالًا	جَمَعَ	الَّذِيۡ
counts it over	and	wealth	amasses	Who

2. Who amasses wealth and counts it over,

يَحۡسَبُ اَنَّ مَالَهٗۤ اَخۡلَدَهٗ ۚ ٣

هٗ	اَخۡلَدَ	هٗ	مَالَ	اَنَّ	يَحۡسَبُ
him	will make live for ever	his	wealth	that	He thinks

3. He thinks his wealth will make him live for ever!

كَلَّا لَيُنۡۢبَذَنَّ فِي الۡحُطَمَةِ ۖ ٤

الۡحُطَمَةِ	فِي	يُنۡۢبَذَنَّ	لَ	كَلَّا
the Crushing Torment	Into	he will be thrown	surely	By no means

4. By no means! Surely, he will be thrown into the Crushing Torment.

وَمَاۤ اَدۡرٰىكَ مَا الۡحُطَمَةُ ؕ ٥

الۡحُطَمَةُ	مَا	كَ	اَدۡرٰ	مَاۤ	وَ
the Crushing Torment	what (is)	you	will make understand	what	And

5. And what will make you understand what the Crushing Torment is?

نَارُ اللّٰهِ الۡمُوۡقَدَةُ ۙ ٦

الۡمُوۡقَدَةُ	اللّٰهِ	نَارُ
which (is) kindled	(of) God	Fire

6. (It is) Fire of God that is kindled!

الَّتِيۡ تَطَّلِعُ عَلَى الۡاَفۡـِٕدَةِ ؕ ٧

الۡاَفۡـِٕدَةِ	عَلَى	تَطَّلِعُ	الَّتِيۡ
the hearts	over	leaps	That which

7. That leaps over the (criminal) hearts!

إِنَّهَا عَلَيْهِم مُّؤْصَدَةٌ ﴿٨﴾				
مُّؤْصَدَةٌ	هِمْ	عَلَيْ	هَا	إِنَّ
closed	them	upon	it (is)	Verily
8. Verily, it is closed upon them,				

فِي عَمَدٍ مُّمَدَّدَةٍ ﴿٩﴾		
مُّمَدَّدَةٍ	عَمَدٍ	فِي
outstretched	columns	In
9. In columns outstretched.		

104 (c) Outline Structure of Sūrah al-Humazah

The *sūrah* makes its point in three stages:

A. **[*Āyāt* 1-*3*] This is the character of a worshipper of wealth.**

As manifest through his/her expressions, this person loves wealth but fails to respect his/her fellow servants of God. The lovers of God are concerned with their fellow human beings. They respect everyone.

B. **[*Āyāt* 4-7] The central *āyāt* contain the main theme:**

Love and remembrance of God bring real peace of mind and soul, while love of wealth creates hatred of fellow human beings and results in Anger of God. The **lover of wealth chose *NārAllāh* (Fire/Anger of God) instead of *NūrAllāh* (Light of God).**

C. **[*Āyah* 8 & *āyah 9*] The above is the psychology of a stingy person:**

However, if one's wealth goes on increasing, it will not compensate the narrowness of one's heart. Likewise, one will feel even more congested with tall, stretching pillars of Hell around oneself.

(Each increase in one's bank balance will make these pillars taller.)

104 (d) Sūrah al-Humazah
Understanding and Interpretation

The worshippers of wealth do not have any respect or concern for their fellow humans. They are only concerned with making more and more wealth. However, as they accumulate more wealth neglecting their duty to their fellow human being - thus adding more fuel to the Hellfir - they increase Divine Wrath.

The worshippers of wealth think wealth can buy everything and it will allow them to live eternally. However, their increasing wealth will bring no real peace of mind even in this life. And in the Hereafter, the Fire of Hell will leap over the criminals' hearts.

And their increasing bank account will only further stretch the Columns of Hell – further closing the Fire over the misers, bringing more congestion.

For the 'closed Fire of Hell' also consider *āyah* 90: 20. It is closed upon people who committed *kufr*. In the context of the *Sūrah al-Balad* (90) these are the stingy people who did not share their wealth with the needy.

Chapter Twenty Four

105 (a) Sūrah al Fīl

سُورَةُ الْفِيلِ

بِسْمِ اللّٰهِ الرَّحْمٰنِ الرَّحِيْمِ

اَلَمْ تَرَ كَيْفَ فَعَلَ رَبُّكَ بِاَصْحٰبِ الْفِيْلِ ﴿١﴾ اَلَمْ يَجْعَلْ كَيْدَهُمْ

فِيْ تَضْلِيْلٍ ﴿٢﴾ وَّاَرْسَلَ عَلَيْهِمْ طَيْرًا اَبَابِيْلَ ﴿٣﴾ تَرْمِيْهِمْ بِحِجَارَةٍ

مِّنْ سِجِّيْلٍ ﴿٤﴾ فَجَعَلَهُمْ كَعَصْفٍ مَّاْكُوْلٍ ﴿٥﴾

105 (b) Word by word translation of Sūrah al-Fīl

اَلَمْ تَرَ كَيْفَ فَعَلَ رَبُّكَ بِاَصْحٰبِ الْفِيْلِ ۝١

الْفِيْلِ	اَصْحٰبِ	بِ	كَ	رَبُّ	فَعَلَ	كَيْفَ	تَرَ	اَلَمْ
(of) the elephants	the companions	with	your	Lord	dealt	how	you see	Did not?

1. Did you not see (O Prophet!): 'how your Lord dealt with the Army of the Elephants?'

اَلَمْ يَجْعَلْ كَيْدَهُمْ فِيْ تَضْلِيْلٍ ۝٢

تَضْلِيْلٍ	فِيْ	هُمْ	كَيْدَ	يَجْعَلْ	اَلَمْ
utter failure	in	their	plan	He make	Did not?

2. Did He not make their (treacherous) plan an utter failure!

وَّاَرْسَلَ عَلَيْهِمْ طَيْرًا اَبَابِيْلَ ۝٣

اَبَابِيْلَ	طَيْرًا	هِمْ	عَلَيْ	اَرْسَلَ	وَّ
birds	flying	them	against	He sent	And

3. And (God) sent against them flights of birds!

تَرْمِيْهِمْ بِحِجَارَةٍ مِّنْ سِجِّيْلٍ ۝٤

سِجِّيْلٍ	مِّنْ	حِجَارَةٍ	بِ	هِمْ	تَرْمِيْ
registered (entries)	(with)	stones	with	them	These were striking

4. (These birds) were striking them with stones according to registered entries.

فَجَعَلَهُمْ كَعَصْفٍ مَّاْكُوْلٍ ۝٥

مَّاْكُوْلٍ	عَصْفٍ	كَ	هُمْ	جَعَلَ	فَ
eaten	straw	like	them	He made	Thus

5. Thus (God) made them like eaten up straw!

105 (c) Outline Structure of Sūrah al-Fīl

The *sūrah* makes its point in three stages:

A. **[*Āyah* 1] says to the Prophet by way of consolation:**
Why are you so worried at the envious plans of these opponents?
Do you not know how God protected this House of God in the past?

B. **[*Āyāt* 2-4] explain the Divine Action in three stages:**
Āyah 2: all their plans failed.
Āyah 3: Divine help comes from unseen corners.
Āyah 4: Every shot was pre-registered.
(A whole shower of stone-pebbles was well-calculated.)

C. **[*Āyāt* 5] The concluding ā*yah* remarks:**
The enemy was, thereby, completely routed.

105 (d) Sūrah al-Fīl
Understanding and Interpretation

The *sūrah* makes the following point:

The Prophet should not be worried at the envious plans of the unjust opponents, as if God is saying to the Prophet: 'This should not be your headache! You just take care of the job assigned to you. I will deal with My enemies just as I did earlier with the People of Elephants who invaded the House of God in Makkah.'

The plan to destroy the *Ka'bah* utterly failed when Divine Punishment came from unforeseen corners.

Each step in this Divine Action Plan was very well computerized – even this was predetermined which stone will hit whose head. The unjust aggressor was totally routed!

The *sūrah* suggests that the Prophet should focus on the work which is assigned to him with complete peace of mind. It is so because God Himself has taken the responsibility. God has promised to protect his Quranic Movement against all aggressors who unjustly stand in its way.(73: 11).

Chapter Twenty Five

106 (a) Sūrah al-Quraysh

سُورَةُ قُرَيْشٍ

بِسْمِ ٱللَّهِ ٱلرَّحْمَٰنِ ٱلرَّحِيمِ

لِإِيلَٰفِ قُرَيْشٍ ١ إِۦلَٰفِهِمْ رِحْلَةَ ٱلشِّتَآءِ وَٱلصَّيْفِ ٢ فَلْيَعْبُدُوا۟ رَبَّ
هَٰذَا ٱلْبَيْتِ ٣ ٱلَّذِىٓ أَطْعَمَهُم مِّن جُوعٍ وَءَامَنَهُم مِّنْ خَوْفٍۭ ٤

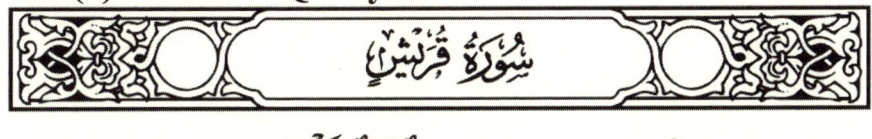

106 (b) Word by word translation of Sūrah Quraysh

لِإِيلَٰفِ قُرَيْشٍ ①		
قُرَيْشٍ	إِيلَٰفِ	لِ
(of) the Quresh	taming	For
1. For the taming of the Quraysh.		

إِۦلَٰفِهِمْ رِحْلَةَ الشِّتَآءِ وَالصَّيْفِ ②					
الصَّيْفِ	وَ	الشِّتَاءِ	رِحْلَةَ	هِمْ	الٰفِ
summer	and	(in) winter	the journey of caravans	them	(for) taming
2. For taming them with the caravans set forth in winter and summer.					

فَلْيَعْبُدُوا رَبَّ هَٰذَا الْبَيْتِ ③					
الْبَيْتِ	هٰذَا	رَبَّ	يَعْبُدُوا	لْ	فَ
House	this	the Lord (of)	worship	(they) should	So
3. So, they also should worship the Lord of this House,					

الَّذِيٓ أَطْعَمَهُمْ مِّنْ جُوعٍ وَّآمَنَهُمْ مِّنْ خَوْفٍ ④									
خَوْفٍ	مِّنْ	هُمْ	اٰمَنَ	وَّ	جُوْعٍ	مِّنْ	هُمْ	أَطْعَمَ	الَّذِيٓ
fear	in	them	secured	and	hunger	In	them	fed	One Who
4. Who fed them against hunger and gave them security from fear.									

106 (c) Outline Structure of Sūrah Quraysh

The *sūrah* makes its point in four stages:

A. **[*Āyah* 1] introduces the subject**
The *sūrah* deals with Special Divine Favor to Quraysh
and with the Divine expectation that they return thanks.

B. **[*Āyah* 2] explains the mode:** How the above Special Divine Favor to them actually operated.

C. **[*Āyah* 3] underlines what Quraysh should do in return.**
This Special Divine Favor was due to their being care-taker and neighbors of The House of God in Makkah. Now they should fulfill the purpose for which The House of God was built.

D. **[*Āyah* 4] explains the point of Divine Blessing in the light of its historical perspective:** The *āyah* implicitly refers to the *du'ā* (prayer) of Abraham and Ishmael which they made when they were raising the walls of The House of God in Makkah. (2:126-129,152)

As if God says, 'I have done my part; you have to do your part too.'

106 (d) Sūrah Quraysh
Understanding and Interpretation

Divine Love is looking for a positive response, by way of thanksgiving, from the neighbors of the House of God in Makkah!

It is a very special case:

Masjid al-Ḥarām is the spiritual center of The International *Tawḥīdic* Movement (2:124-131), established by Abraham and his son Ishmael. The Quraysh who live in the vicinity of this House of God are Children of Ishmael. God granted them a very special favor, by way of security and sustenance, for which Abraham had also made a prayer (2:126).

However, Abraham, had a wish that his progeny continues his *tawḥīdic* mission, and a messenger of God is born in his progeny who teaches them the Book and guides their spiritual and moral development (2: 127-129). The Prophet is the answer to Abraham's prayer.

Now, the Prophet is inviting the Quraysh to the tawḥīdic mission for which Abraham and Ishmael built the House of God and God is looking for their positive response.

Chapter Twenty Six

107 (a) Sūrah al-Mā‘ūn

سُوْرَةُ الْمَاعُوْنِ

بِسْمِ اللّٰهِ الرَّحْمٰنِ الرَّحِيْمِ

أَرَءَيْتَ الَّذِيْ يُكَذِّبُ بِالدِّيْنِ ﴿١﴾ فَذٰلِكَ الَّذِيْ يَدُعُّ الْيَتِيْمَ ﴿٢﴾ وَلَا
يَحُضُّ عَلٰى طَعَامِ الْمِسْكِيْنِ ﴿٣﴾ فَوَيْلٌ لِّلْمُصَلِّيْنَ ﴿٤﴾ الَّذِيْنَ هُمْ عَنْ
صَلَاتِهِمْ سَاهُوْنَ ﴿٥﴾ الَّذِيْنَ هُمْ يُرَآءُوْنَ ﴿٦﴾ وَيَمْنَعُوْنَ الْمَاعُوْنَ ﴿٧﴾

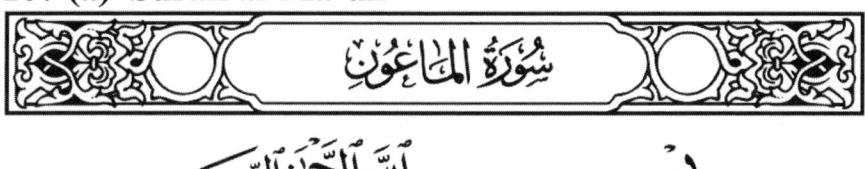

107 (b) Word by word translation of Sūrah al-Ma'ūn

أَرَءَيْتَ الَّذِي يُكَذِّبُ بِالدِّيْنِ ①

الدِّيْنِ	بِ	يُكَذِّبُ	الَّذِيْ	رَءَيْتَ	أَ
the Religion	to	gives lies	one who	you see	Did

1. Did you see the person who gives lie (violently rejects it, saying 'it is all a lie') to the Religion?

فَذٰلِكَ الَّذِيْ يَدُعُّ الْيَتِيْمَ ②

الْيَتِيْمَ	يَدُعُّ	الَّذِيْ	ذٰلِكَ	فَ
the orphans	repulses	one who	that (is)	So

2. So, that is the one who repulses the orphan!

وَلَا يَحُضُّ عَلٰى طَعَامِ الْمِسْكِيْنِ ③

الْمِسْكِيْنِ	طَعَامِ	عَلٰى	يَحُضُّ	لَا	وَ
(of) the poor	feeding	to	urge (others)	does not	And

3. And urges not the feeding of the poor!

فَوَيْلٌ لِّلْمُصَلِّيْنَ ④

الْمُصَلِّيْنَ	لِّ	وَيْلٌ	فَ
those who pray	lo	woe	So

4. So, woe to, (those) people who pray (offer *ṣalāh*)

الَّذِيْنَ هُمْ عَنْ صَلَاتِهِمْ سَاهُوْنَ ⑤

سَاهُوْنَ	هِمْ	صَلٰوة	عَنْ	هُمْ	الَّذِيْنَ
(are) heedless	their	worship	of	(they)	Those who

5. (But) who are heedless of their worship (unaware of their *ṣalāh* i.e., do not know what *ṣalāh* is?)

الَّذِيْنَ هُمْ يُرَآءُوْنَ ⑥

يُرَاءُوْنَ	هُمْ	الَّذِيْنَ
would be seen	(they)	Those who

6. Who would be seen (at worship).

وَيَمْنَعُوْنَ الْمَاعُوْنَ ⑦

الْمَاعُوْنَ	يَمْنَعُوْنَ	وَ
(if asked for) small favor	will refuse	And

107 (c) Outline Structure of Sūrah al-Ma'ūn

The *sūrah* makes its point in four stages:

A. [***Āyah* 1**] introduces the subject:
Who are the opponents - *the people who say 'this is all a lie'?*
If you know who are the people that stand in the way of the Religion, then you can understand why they are doing so.

B. [***Āyah* 2 & *āyah* 3**] *together provide the answer:*
These are the same people who are unconcerned with the plight of the alienated or marginalized sections of human society. They are unconcerned with the establishment of a system that would eliminate poverty or hunger.

They may look like very religious people. However, they are unable to appreciate the way the Religion emphasizes their duty to the deprived and marginalized sections of human society.

C. [***Āyāt* 4-6**] remove the misunderstanding of the simple-minded who wonder why some people who, otherwise, look very religious are standing in the way of the Religion.

These central āyāt underline: False religiosity is doomed. Worship is not a cultural function. If hearts are devoid of the presence of God, the traditional prayer is of no value, however impressive it may look from the outside!

D. [***Āyah* 7**] *concludes:*
What good is their religion if they would not help the needy even with a small act of kindness!

107 (d) Sūrah al-Mā'ūn
Understanding and Interpretation

The sūrah repudiates pseudo-religiosity. It differentiates the true religiosity from the false religiosity.

The first *āyah* of the *sūrah* raises the question: *Who are the opponents* of the Religion? Why do they feel so threatened? It is a very meaningful question because quite a few of them look like very religious people.

The *sūrah* answers that these are the people who do not believe that they have any duty toward the down-trodden or alienated sections of society, which is the Religion's main concern. One should not be deceived by their worship (*ṣalāh)* of God, which is merely a public show; otherwise, their hearts are devoid of any real consciousness of God. *Such worshippers are doomed!*

The Religion straightens a person's relationship with God The Most Merciful, Who is *Rabb al-'alamin* (Lord/Sustainer of the whole world). Quite naturally, as a servant of God comes closer and closer to his/her Lord, consciousness of one's social obligations that are duties from God also grows.

Chapter Twenty Seven

108 (a) Sūrah al-Kauthar

سُوْرَةُ الْكَوْثَرِ

بِسْمِ اللّٰهِ الرَّحْمٰنِ الرَّحِيْمِ

اِنَّآ اَعْطَيْنٰكَ الْكَوْثَرَ ۝١ فَصَلِّ لِرَبِّكَ وَانْحَرْ ۝٢

اِنَّ شَانِئَكَ هُوَ الْاَبْتَرُ ۝٣

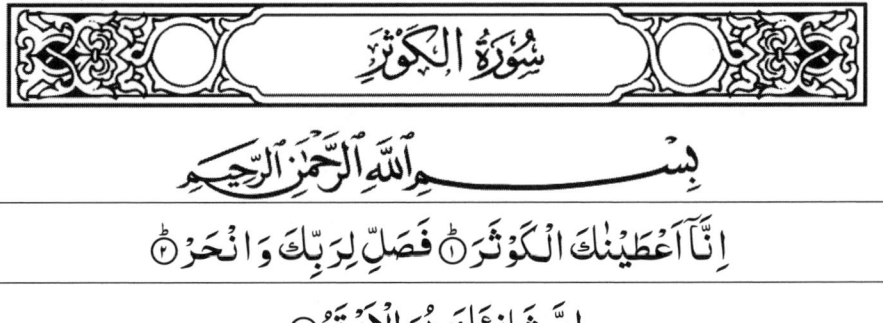

108 (b) Word by word translation of Sūrah al-Kawthar

إِنَّآ أَعْطَيْنَٰكَ ٱلْكَوْثَرَ ۝١

الْكَوْثَرَ	كَ	أَعْطَيْنَا	إِنَّآ
al-Kawthar	you	We have given	Verily We

1. Verily, We have given you (O Prophet,) al-Kawthar (The Abundance of Good)

فَصَلِّ لِرَبِّكَ وَٱنْحَرْ ۝٢

انْحَرْ	وَ	كَ	رَبِّ	لِ	صَلِّ	فَ
sacrifice	and	your	Lord	for	pray	Therefore

2. Therefore, pray (offer *ṣalāh*) to your Lord and sacrifice.

إِنَّ شَانِئَكَ هُوَ ٱلْأَبْتَرُ ۝٣

الْأَبْتَرُ	هُوَ	كَ	شَانِئَ	إِنَّ
(is) lopped off	he	you	one who hates	Surely

3. Surely, one who hates you is the one that is lopped off.

108 (c) Outline Structure of Sūrah al-Kawthar

The *sūrah* makes its point in three stages:

A. **[*Āyah* 1] Proclamation from the Divine Authority:**

'We have granted you (O Prophet!) the *Kauthar*, i.e. something whose blessings will go on increasing!'

The Understanding of the Quran will grow with the progress in human knowledge. As humanity will strive to follow its guidance, the whole world will be filled with blessings: peace, progress and prosperity.

B. **[*Āyah* 2] The central ā*yah* explains what the Recipient should therefore,, do:**

i) make *ṣalāh* (a statement full of meaning),
ii) make sacrifice (a statement full of meaning).

C. **[*Āyah* 3]** The concluding ā*yah* tells the Recipient of the *Kauthar* not to worry about the opposition to the Qur'anic Movement: As the movement shall proceed further**, gradually all the opposition will wither away.**

108 (d) Sūrah al-Kawthar
Understanding and Interpretation

(The previous *sūrah* pointed out that false religiosity is doomed. The present *sūrah* underlines that the blessings of true religiosity will go on increasing.)

The revelation of the Qur'an to the Prophet, came at the very end of the prophetic movement. It is an unending source of Divine Blessings. As such, it is the greatest gift from the Creator to the human world. As the believing community will continue its reflections on Divine Signs (Qur'anic *āyāt*), in changing human situations, the growth in human knowledge will help further progress in the Understanding of the Divine Words. And as the believing community continues to follow the Qur'anic guidance, more and more justice, peace, prosperity, and progress will prevail in the human world.

What is important: Prayer is not sufficient. Sacrifice is also a must!

Through prayer and sacrifice the Qur'anic Community maintains a living relationship with the Divine Words.

Thus, the *sūrah* underlines the following *items for action*:

1. 'establish prayer'; this has three dimensions:

   i. thanking God for guiding us

   Offering of *ṣalāh* (prayer) is a way of giving thanks to God for this great gift of God to humankind

   ii. *ṣalāh* stands for practically submitting to God

   establishment of *ṣalāh* is a symbol for establishment of Qur'anic system in human life

   iii. mainly in *ṣalāh* itself listening to Divine Speech and pondering over Divine Words is an important part. These are most important moments for reflection on Qur'anic *Āyāt.*

2. offer sacrifice, that is, continuing the striving in the path of Quranic Movement with perseverance and steadfastness.

   The surah concludes: as the Quranic Movement proceeds further all hatred will wither away!

Chapter Twenty Eight

109 (a) Sūrah al-Kāfirūn

سُورَةُ الكَافِرُونَ

بِسْمِ ٱللَّهِ ٱلرَّحْمَٰنِ ٱلرَّحِيمِ

قُلْ يَٰٓأَيُّهَا ٱلْكَٰفِرُونَ ١ لَآ أَعْبُدُ مَا تَعْبُدُونَ ٢ وَلَآ أَنتُمْ عَٰبِدُونَ مَآ
أَعْبُدُ ٣ وَلَآ أَنَا۠ عَابِدٌ مَّا عَبَدتُّمْ ٤ وَلَآ أَنتُمْ عَٰبِدُونَ مَآ أَعْبُدُ ٥
لَكُمْ دِينُكُمْ وَلِيَ دِينِ ٦

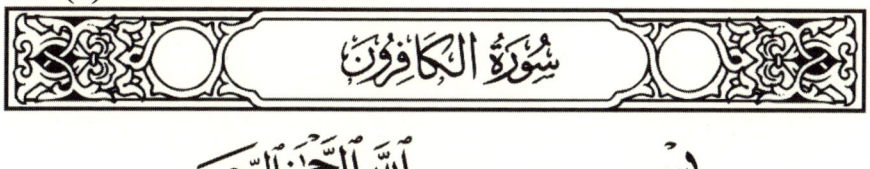

109 (b) Word by word translation of Sūrah al-Kāfirūn

قُلْ يٰٓاَيُّهَا الْكٰفِرُوْنَ ۙ١

الْكٰفِرُوْنَ	يٰٓاَيُّهَا	قُلْ
Disbelievers!	O!	Say

1. Tell (them):' O Disbelievers!' (People who rejected my call)

لَآ اَعْبُدُ مَا تَعْبُدُوْنَ ۙ٢

تَعْبُدُوْنَ	مَا	اَعْبُدُ	لَآ
you worship	what	I worship	do not

2. 'I do not worship what you worship.'

وَلَآ اَنْتُمْ عٰبِدُوْنَ مَآ اَعْبُدُ ۚ٣

اَعْبُدُ	مَآ	عٰبِدُوْنَ	اَنْتُمْ	لَآ	وَ
I worship	what	(are going to) worship	you	nor	And

3. 'Nor, are you going to worship what I worship.'

وَلَآ اَنَا عَابِدٌ مَّا عَبَدْتُّمْ ۙ٤

عَبَدْتُّمْ	مَّا	عَابِدٌ	اَنَا	لَآ	وَ
you worshiped	what	(am going to) worship	I	neither	And

4. Again! 'Neither am I going to worship what you have been worshipping.'

وَلَآ اَنْتُمْ عٰبِدُوْنَ مَآ اَعْبُدُ ۗ٥

اَعْبُدُ	مَآ	عٰبِدُوْنَ	اَنْتُمْ	لَآ	وَ
I worship	what	((am going to) worship	you	nor	And

5. 'Nor, are you going to worship what I worship.'

لَكُمْ دِيْنُكُمْ وَلِيَ دِيْنِ ٦

دِيْنِ	يَ	لِ	وَ	كُمْ	دِيْنُ	كُمْ	لَ
my religion	me	for	and	your	religion	you	For

6. '(So,) for you, your religion; and for me, my religion.'

109 (c) Outline Structure of Sūrah al-Kāfirūn

The *sūrah* makes its point in three stages:

A. **[*Āyah*–1]** *The very first āyah introduces the subject:*

What to say to those who rejected our message and who are putting *pressure upon us to leave our Tawḥīdic mission altogether or make some adjustment in our stand.*

In fact, they have already rejected our message, but they are eager to talk to us in order to make a bargain.

B. **[*Āyāt* 2–5]** Tell them**:** *no good shall come out of our trying to convert each other:*

Āyah 2 and *āyah* 3 state: **we have fundamental religious differences.** '(When I, i.e., the Prophet, received the Divine Guidance that God and **God alone is to be worshiped**), as your well-wisher, I invited you to it, but now it is quite clear that you are not going to change your religious position.'

Āyah 4 and *āyah* 5 repeat, it is quite clear that each of the two parties is quite firm in its stand. No one is going to change, how hard you try that I change my religion or I try that you change your religion.

C. **[*Āyah* 6]** *Peaceful co-existence is possible:*

The present conflict can be resolved, if we agree that every individual is free to choose his/her religion and that we should not put any kind of pressure on anyone to change one's religion.

109 (d) Sūrah al-Kāfirūn

Understanding and Interpretation

There should be no compromise in the fundamental principles of the Religion. If it becomes clear that the addressees have in fact already decided that they are not going to believe, then there is no use in continuing the argument with them.

However, everyone is free to follow one's own religion, and there should be no coercion of any kind.

Calling to believe is, in fact, an invitation to thinking; however, if it is degenerating into an unfriendly discussion or if some kind of pressure is being applied by any party, then it is better to discontinue this dialogue. Say to the other party: '**You follow your way. I will follow my way. In spite of differences in our approaches, we can live peacefully in the same society.** Freedom of religion is essential.We want it for ourselves. And we give it to others.'

The disagreement is between two ways of thinking. They are so radically different! However, the Qur'an says these are 'two ways of worshipping.'

The Qur'an divides humankind into two camps:

1. Worshippers of One God, who believe that God alone is the Lord of Humankind and that there should be no lordship of human beings over human beings.

2. Those who have other masters - other gods (*ilāh*) or lords. In one form or the other; they support lordship of human beings over human beings.

Chapter Twenty Nine

110 (a) Sūrah an-Naṣr

سُورَةُ النَّصْرِ

بِسْمِ ٱللَّهِ ٱلرَّحْمَٰنِ ٱلرَّحِيمِ

إِذَا جَآءَ نَصْرُ اللهِ وَ الْفَتْحُ ١ وَرَاَيْتَ النَّاسَ يَدْخُلُونَ فِي دِينِ اللهِ
اَفْوَاجًا ٢ فَسَبِّحْ بِحَمْدِ رَبِّكَ وَ اسْتَغْفِرْهُ اِنَّهُ كَانَ تَوَّابًا ٣

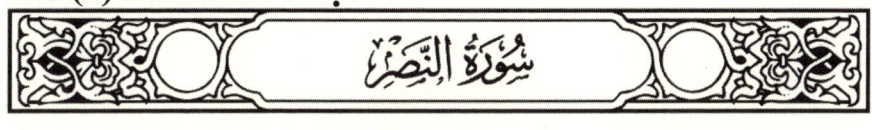

110 (b) Word by word translation of Sūrah An-Naṣr

اِذَا جَآءَ نَصۡرُ اللّٰهِ وَالۡفَتۡحُ ۙ①					
الۡفَتۡحُ	وَ	اللّٰهِ	نَصۡرُ	جَآءَ	اِذَا
the Victory	and	(of) God	help	arrives	When
1. When the Divine Help arrives and the Victory (is achieved),					

وَرَاَيۡتَ النَّاسَ يَدۡخُلُوۡنَ فِىۡ دِيۡنِ اللّٰهِ اَفۡوَاجًا ۙ②							
اَفۡوَاجًا ۙ	اللّٰهِ	دِيۡنِ	فِىۡ	يَدۡخُلُوۡنَ	النَّاسَ	رَاَيۡتَ	وَ
in large groups	(of) God	The Religion	into	entering	the people	you see	And
2. And you see people entering into the Religion of God in large groups,							

فَسَبِّحۡ بِحَمۡدِ رَبِّكَ وَاسۡتَغۡفِرۡهُ								
هُ	اسۡتَغۡفِرۡ	وَ	كَ	رَبِّ	حَمۡدِ	بِ	سَبِّحۡ	فَ
His	seek forgiveness	and	of your	Lord	praise	with	glorify	So
3. So, glorify your Lord with His praise, and seek His forgiveness.								

اِنَّهٗ كَانَ تَوَّابًا ③			
تَوَّابًا	كَانَ	هٗ	اِنَّ
Oft-Retruning	is	He	Verily
Verily, God is Oft-Returning!			

110 (c) Outline Structure of Sūrah An-Naṣr

The *sūrah* makes its points in three stages:

A. **[*Āyah* 1] implicitly, introduces two questions:**
What should one expect when the **Help of God brings Victory?**
What should the Prophet (and the believers) do then?

B. **[*Āyah* 2] answers the first question:**
(The downfall of unjust power will open the door for)
large groups of people entering into God's Religion.

C. **[*Āyah* 3] is concerned with the main (second) question:**
It explains, after the Victory is achieved, what the Prophet (and the believers) should do.

110 (d) Sūrah An-Naṣr
Understanding and Interpretation

The Context for Victory and Help of God:

Sūrah An-Naṣr* (110) answers the question: *How should the believers celebrate victory* when it comes? But why did the question of victory arise in the context of the preceding *sūrahs?

In fact, the ***promise*** of victory was already implicit in Divine consolation to the Prophet in *Sūrahal-Fīl* (105), which was succeeded by Divine reminding to Quraysh of their duty in *Sūrah Quraysh* (106), and the clarification in *Sūrah al-Mā'ūn* (107) and *Sūrah al-Kawthar* (108) that false religiosity is doomed and that ultimately the Qur'anic Movement, which is reviving true religiosity, will prevail.

However, it seems that the preceding *Sūrah, al-Kāfirūn* (109), also contains the following implicit suggestion: If believers will combine two qualities in their conduct - **truthfulness and mutual respect of their fellow human beings** - sooner or later the **victory** will follow.

Victory and the Help of God are mutually connected:

The believers know that the Victory will not come without the Help of God. If Victory is delayed it means God is withholding the *Naṣr* (Help of God). So they are waiting for the *Naṣr* and making *du'ā* for it. At the same time the believers are seeking forgiveness of God; perhaps *Naṣr* is delayed due to some of their shortcomings.

The central theme of the *Sūrah An-Naṣr* (110)

The *Sūrah*, implicitly, suggests that Help of God and thereby **Victory is on its way.**

However, the *sūrah* is mainly concerned with the question**: What shall the believers do when Help of God arrives and thereby Victory is achieved?**

When arrogant and unjust people attain victory, they act cruelly and transcend all legal and moral boundaries. The *sūrah,* therefore, underlines that, on such occasions, the coduct of the virtuous believers, should be very different from those criminals. This is why, in 2:58-59, an earlier community of believers was criticized for failing the test**. The present *sūrah* underlines that, when Victory arrives, believers should remember God more and more.** They should glorify God by way of praising and thanking God. They should not forget that **it is God's Help which brought the Victory**.

At the same time, the believers should **be critical** of their own performance and **seek more and more of God's forgiveness for their shortcomings.**

In brief, the believers should maintain **humility, gratitude and self-criticism and make more and more remembrance of God.**

Chapter Thirty

111 (a) Sūrah al-Masad

سُورَةُ الْمَسَدِ

بِسْمِ اللّٰهِ الرَّحْمٰنِ الرَّحِيْمِ

تَبَّتْ يَدَآ اَبِيْ لَهَبٍ وَّتَبَّ ۝١ مَآ اَغْنٰى عَنْهُ مَالُهٗ وَمَا كَسَبَ ۝٢ سَيَصْلٰى نَارًا
ذَاتَ لَهَبٍ ۝٣ وَّامْرَاَتُهٗ حَمَّالَةَ الْحَطَبِ ۝٤ فِيْ جِيْدِهَا حَبْلٌ مِّنْ مَّسَدٍ ۝٥

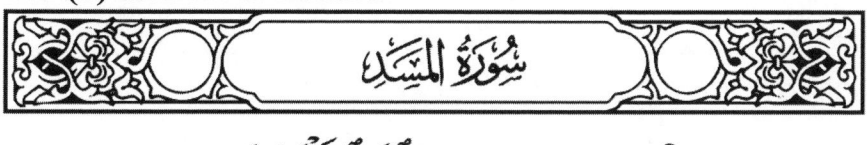

111 (b) Word by word translation of Sūrah al-Masad

تَبَّتْ يَدَآ اَبِيْ لَهَبٍ وَّتَبَّ ۝١

تَبَّ	وَّ	لَهَبٍ	اَبِيْ	يَدَآ	تَبَّتْ
he preshied	and	Lahab	Abu	hands (of)	Perished

1. Perished both the hands of Abu Lahab and perished he.

مَآ اَغْنٰى عَنْهُ مَالُهٗ وَمَا كَسَبَ ۝٢

كَسَبَ	مَا	وَ	هٗ	مَالُ	عَنْهُ	اَغْنٰى	مَآ
earned	what	and	his	wealth	(to) him	benefited	Not

2. His wealth availed him not, nor what he earned.

سَيَصْلٰى نَارًا ذَاتَ لَهَبٍ ۝٣

لَهَبٍ	ذَاتَ	نَارًا	يَصْلٰى	سَ
a flame	of (having)	(in) a fire	he shall roast	Soon

3. Soon, he shall roast at a flaming fire.

وَّامْرَاَتُهٗ حَمَّالَةَ الْحَطَبِ ۝٤

الْحَطَبِ	هٗ	حَمَّالَ	هٗ	امْرَاَتُ	وَّ
of the firewood	its	the carrier	his	wife	And

4. And (also) his wife, the carrier of the firewood.

فِيْ جِيْدِهَا حَبْلٌ مِّنْ مَّسَدٍ ۝٥

مَّسَدٍ	مِّنْ	حَبْلٌ	هَا	جِيْدِ	فِيْ
palm-fiber	of	a rope	her	neck	around

5. Around her neck a rope of palm-fiber.

111 (c) Outline Structure of Sūrah al-Masad

The *sūrah* makes its points in three stages:

A. **[*Āyah* 1] introduces the subject:**

(It picks up the concrete example of an enemy of the Religion of God to show the consequences of such conduct).

Abu Lahab is doomed and his power is ruined.

B. **[*Āyah* 2 and *āyah* 3] present the central theme of the *sūrah*.**

Even in this life, Abu Lahab's wealth and his position in society, on the basis of which and for love of which he acted enviously against the Religion, did not help him. And in the Hereafter too when Abu Lahab will enter into the Hellfire to live there permanently, he will find himself helpless .

C. **[*Āyah* 4 and *āyah* 5] add: The same will be the fate of his life companion.**

Abu Lahab's wife, who was behind her spouse in all his crimes, is doomed too. In Hell, her precious necklace is turned into a strong rope to carry the fuel for the fire of Hell for herself and for her husband.

111 (d) Sūrah al-Masad

Understanding and Interpretation

The *sūrah* pinpoints Abu Lahab as the person who stood in the way of the Qur'anic Movement. However, when Divine Punishment came, neither his wealth nor his position in society could save him.

The concluding *āyah* of *Sūrah al-Kawthar* (108) implicitly remarked: those whose hearts are full of heatred for the Phrophet and who are unjustly opposing the Religion of God have no future. Earlier, *Sūrah al-Mā'ūn* (107) underlined who are the main opponents of the Qur'anic Movement that is reviving the True Religiosity. Abu Lahab shares the qualities of those who represent false religiosity and who are doomed.

Sūrah al-Masad (111) also makes it clear that Abu Lahab's spouse, who was behind his crimes, will share the punishment. In the place of her precious necklace, she will have a rope around her neck to carry the firewood, to add - for both of them - more fuel to the Fire of Hell.

Chapter Thirty One

112 (a) Sūrah al-Ikhlāṣ

سُورَةُ الإِخْلَاصِ

بِسْمِ اللَّهِ الرَّحْمَٰنِ الرَّحِيمِ

قُلْ هُوَ اللَّهُ أَحَدٌ ﴿١﴾ اللَّهُ الصَّمَدُ ﴿٢﴾ لَمْ يَلِدْ وَلَمْ يُولَدْ ﴿٣﴾

وَلَمْ يَكُن لَّهُ كُفُوًا أَحَدٌ ﴿٤﴾

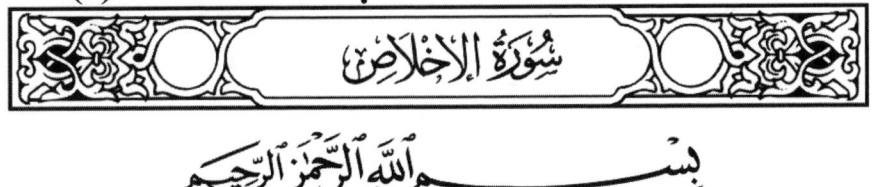

112 (b) Word by word translation of Sūrah al-Ikhlāṣ

قُلْ هُوَ اللّٰهُ اَحَدٌ ۚ ١

اَحَدٌ	اللّٰهُ	هُوَ	قُلْ
The Only One	God	He (is)	Say

1. Say: 'He is God, The Only One.

اَللّٰهُ الصَّمَدُ ۚ ٢

الصَّمَدُ	اَللّٰهُ
(is) the *Ṣamad*	God

2. God is the *Ṣamad* (The Being on Whom every being is dependent, and is independent of every being).

لَمْ يَلِدْ ۙ وَلَمْ يُوْلَدْ ۙ ٣

يُوْلَدْ	لَمْ	وَ	يَلِدْ	لَمْ
He is begotten	nor	(and)	He begets	Neither

3. (God) never had (or will have) a son or a daughter nor (God) had a father or a mother.

وَلَمْ يَكُنْ لَّهٗ كُفُوًا اَحَدٌ ٤

اَحَدٌ	كُفُوًا	لَّهٗ	يَكُنْ	لَمْ	وَ
anyone	a match	(to) Him	is	not	And

4. 'No one, at all, is like (God). (No one can be a match to God)

112 (c) Outline Structure of Sūrah al-Ikhlāṣ

The *sūrah* makes its points in four stages:

A. [*Āyah* 1] **The introductory** ***āyah*** **states in clear terms that God is only one.** Any effort to bring plurality or duality in the Being of God is not permitted at all.

B. [*Āyah* 2] states the essential point explaining the nature of the Being of God: **God is the** ***Ṣamad*** **- the Being upon Whom all beings depend and Who does not depend upon anyone else.**

C. [*Āyah* 3] **clarifies that it is confusing to use, in connection with God, a language that we use to designate human relations**. God is not father or mother of someone; nor is God son or daughter of any one.

D. [*Āyah* 4] **Concludes: No being is like (matching) God!**

112 (d) Sūrah al-Ikhlāṣ
Understanding and Interpretation

The Qur'an has been calling the people to join the community of *Allāh's* (God's) loyal (sincere) servants. However, the people are confused about the Being of God. It is required that this confusion is removed through a simple, brief and fool-proof statement in the Arabic language.

The *sūrah* explains that God is the Being on whom all other beings depend, and that God does not depend on any other being.

Therefore, the first and the foremost truth about God is that God does not have any duality or plurality in God's Being. There is One and only One God.

The second is a warning concerning the use of anthropomorphic language, which designates relations between and among human beings, which should not be used in God's relationship with *any being whatsoever*. That is, we can not say that God is father or mother of any one or God is son or daughter of any one. Likewise, you can not say God is spouse of anyone. Such propositions will not make any sense, and the use of such a language is the most serious crime against God (Glory be to God!).

In a nutshell, God is a Unique Being: No one is like God.

Chapter Thirty Two

113 (a) Sūrah al-Falaq

سُورَةُ الْفَلَقِ

بِسْمِ اللّٰهِ الرَّحْمٰنِ الرَّحِيْمِ

قُلْ اَعُوْذُ بِرَبِّ الْفَلَقِ ﴿١﴾ مِنْ شَرِّ مَا خَلَقَ ﴿٢﴾ وَمِنْ شَرِّ غَاسِقٍ اِذَا
وَقَبَ ﴿٣﴾ وَمِنْ شَرِّ النَّفّٰثٰتِ فِي الْعُقَدِ ﴿٤﴾ وَمِنْ شَرِّ حَاسِدٍ اِذَا حَسَدَ ﴿٥﴾

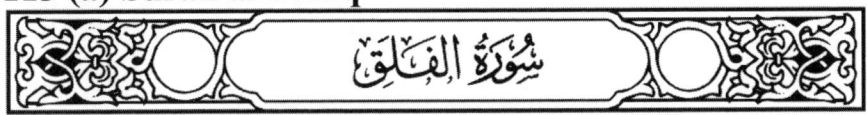

113 (b) Word by word translation of Sūrah al-Falaq

قُلْ اَعُوْذُ بِرَبِّ الْفَلَقِ ﴿١﴾

الْفَلَقِ	رَبِّ	بِ	اَعُوْذُ	قُلْ
(of) daybreak	the Lord	with	I take refuge	Say

1. Say: I take the refuge with the Lord of the Daybreak.

مِنْ شَرِّ مَا خَلَقَ ﴿٢﴾

خَلَقَ	مَا	شَرِّ	مِنْ
He created	(of) what	the evil	From

2. From the evil of what (Lord of the Daybreak /God) created.

وَمِنْ شَرِّ غَاسِقٍ اِذَا وَقَبَ ﴿٣﴾

وَقَبَ	اِذَا	غَاسِقٍ	شَرِّ	مِنْ	وَ
it prevailed	when	(of) darkness	the evil	from	And

3. And from the evil of darkness (of night) when it prevails.

وَمِنْ شَرِّ النَّفّٰثٰتِ فِي الْعُقَدِ ﴿٤﴾

الْعُقَدِ	فِي	النَّفّٰثٰتِ	شَرِّ	مِنْ	وَ
konts	on	of (witches) who blow	the evil	from	And

4. And from the evil of the women (witches) who blow on knots.

وَمِنْ شَرِّ حَاسِدٍ اِذَا حَسَدَ ﴿٥﴾

حَسَدَ	اِذَا	حَاسِدٍ	شَرِّ	مِنْ	وَ
he envies	when	(of)an envier	the evil	from	And

5. And from the evil of an envier when he envies.

113 (c) Outline Structure of Sūrah al-Falaq

The *sūrah* makes its points in three stages:

A. **[*Āyāt* 1-3]** *Introductory āyāt contain the central theme of the sūrah.* Very naturally, with the *coming of the Light of Guidance, the lovers of Darkness will be disturbed* and will strive to prevent the Light of Guidance from spreading. However, everything is in the Hands of God, Who is the Creator of all that exists and Who is bringing the Light.The Prophet and the believers, therefore, need not worry. They should proceed with wisdom and steadfastness, having trust in God and seeking God's Help.

B. **[*Āyah* 4]** explains that ultimately everything being in the Hands of God, *the unjust opponents do not possess any real power. They are like witches* who may try some devious tactics. However, God will protect the believers and they will not be able to harm them.

C. **[*Āyah* 5]** The concluding *āyah* comes back to the central theme and explains *the nature of the real threat, i.e., jealousy amongst various groups which turns into envy:* Satan is full of envy; he wants to show to God that the creation of human beings is futile. Satan is trying to prove that humans are no better than *jinn* who had earlier filled the earth with corruption and bloodshed. Satan wants to show that he was justified in refusing to prostrate to Adam.

Quite often, various groups working for a noble cause become envious of each other. Envy develops among followers of different prophets of God and even within the same believing community. The remedy lies in *du'ā*, that God protects us from the evil of envy.

113 (d) Sūrah al-Falaq
Understanding and Interpretation

The progress of the Qur'anic movement is a threat to the prevailing darkness. Lordship of other than One God is behind the present corruption and mischief in the human world. But if God, Who is bringing this enlightenment, is with you, no one can stop your progress and no one can do any harm to you!

Therefore, have trust in God. Seek God's refuge. God is the Creator of every thing, and every thing is under God's Control.

The unjust opponents are like those malignant persons who are unable to do any physical harm so they turn to witchcraft. However, falsehood can not stand in the face of the Truth.

However, *ḥasad* (jealousy turning to envy) develops between followers of prophets of God and even within this community of believers. It is the greatest threat to the Qur'anic Movement. And behind all these oppositions is *the great envier* (*ḥasid*), Satan, the Enemy of Humankind. *Seek God's protection from all these envies, as you continue to lead the Qur'anic Movement in difficult circumstances.*

Chapter Thirty Three

114 (a) Sūrah an-Nās

سُورَةُ النَّاسِ

بِسْمِ اللَّهِ الرَّحْمَٰنِ الرَّحِيمِ

قُلْ أَعُوذُ بِرَبِّ النَّاسِ ﴿١﴾ مَلِكِ النَّاسِ ﴿٢﴾ إِلَٰهِ النَّاسِ ﴿٣﴾ مِن شَرِّ الْوَسْوَاسِ
الْخَنَّاسِ ﴿٤﴾ الَّذِي يُوَسْوِسُ فِي صُدُورِ النَّاسِ ﴿٥﴾ مِنَ الْجِنَّةِ وَالنَّاسِ ﴿٦﴾

114 (b) Sūrah an-Nās

قُلْ اَعُوْذُ بِرَبِّ النَّاسِ ۝١				
النَّاسِ	رَبِّ	بِ	اَعُوْذُ	قُلْ
(of) humankind	the Lord	with	I take refuge	Say
1. Say: I take refuge with The Lord of Humankind.				

مَلِكِ النَّاسِ ۝٢	
النَّاسِ	مَلِكِ
(of) humankind	The King
2. The King of Humankind,	

اِلٰهِ النَّاسِ ۝٣	
النَّاسِ	اِلٰهِ
(of) humankind	The Deity
3. The Deity of Humankind,	

مِنْ شَرِّ الْوَسْوَاسِ الْخَنَّاسِ ۝٤			
الْخَنَّاسِ	الْوَسْوَاسِ	شَرِّ	مِنْ
sneaky	(of) the whisperer	the evil	From
4. From the evil of the sneaky whisperer,			

الَّذِيْ يُوَسْوِسُ فِيْ صُدُوْرِ النَّاسِ ۝٥				
النَّاسِ	صُدُوْرِ	فِيْ	يُوَسْوِسُ	الَّذِيْ
(of) humandkind	the breast	In	whispers	One who
5. Who whispers in the breasts of humankind,				

مِنَ الْجِنَّةِ وَالنَّاسِ ۝٦			
النَّاسِ	وَ	الْجِنَّةِ	مِنَ
Humandkind	and	Jinn	From
6. From amongst jinn and humankind.			

114 (c) Outline Structure of Sūrah an-Nās

The *sūrah* makes its point in three stages:

A. **[*Āyāt* 1-3] deal with: 'Whose refuge is sought and why?'**

I seek the refuge of **The *Rabb* (Lord) of Humankind**:
God alone is my Sustainer so to God I turn for refuge!
I seek the refuge of **The King of Humankind:**
Unjust people possess no power. The political power which they seem to posses is simply an illusion. If God is with me, no one can hurt me.
I seek the refuge of **The Deity of Humankind.**
As such it is only God who listens to my prayers.

B. **[*Āyah* 4 and *āyah* 5] explain how satanic powers operate and where fighting with Satan takes place.**

Satans play with human psychology; they keep instigating again and again, creating irrational doubts. When we challenge them boldly, they cannot stand against rational argument. They intimidate us, arouse our feelings and sentiments, our greed for power and glory.

C. **[*Āyah* 6] pinpoints the persons 'who do the above satanic activities':**

Quite often, these satans are **invisible**; they act from inside our own beings. But sometimes we can recognize **humans who are working as Satan's agents.**

114 (d) Sūrah an-Nās

Understanding and Interpretation

The *sūrah* is a prayer that God helps us against satanic forces. However, the *sūrah* recommends that during our fight with these forces we should proceed wisely, having full trust in God and disregarding irrational doubts, threats and temptations in our way.

We should not let Satanic forces succeed in playing with our psychological weaknesses. Obviously all power is in the Hand of God. If we have trust in God, these forces will not be able to intimidate us. Likewise, if we remain firm and steadfast, always seeking God's refuge, their temptations and other deceptive techniques will not work.

The Qur'anic Movement is directed toward the fulfillment of Divine Expectations that **humankind becomes one family of God's fellow-servants,** and **there is perfect peace and justice on Earth.** The Great Envier, the Satan, is trying very hard to show that the creation of human beings is futile – that humans are no better than jinn who had, earlier, filled the Earth with corruption and bloodshed. Therefore, seek the refuge of the Lord of Humankind. Pray that God help those who are working for the fulfillment of the mission of God's prophets, so that the purpose of human beings's creation is fulfilled and Satan is totally frustrated in his envious plans.

Seek the refuge of the King of Humankind: Do not be scared of the unjust, arrogant political powers. If God is with you, no one can stand in your way and no one can hurt you!

Turn away from all false gods. Come back to the Real God, the only One Deity. Seek the refuge of the God of Humankind, Who listens to the prayers of all sincere servants.

Chapter Thirty Four

An Overall Look on System underlying *Sūrahs* 85-114

The following contains the author's effort to understand the system underlying the arrangement of the last thirty *sūrahs* of the Qur'an, studied in this book. These thirty *sūrahs* can be grouped into following five subgroups:

(I) ***Sūrah al-Burūj* (85) and *Sūrah aṭ-Ṭāriq* (86):** These two *sūrahs* address a difficult situation in which the unjust people are persecuting helpless believers. The Qur'an gives assurance of Divine help to the believers and issues warning to the criminals so that they make *tawbah*, i.e., repent and correct themselves.

(II) ***Sūrah al-A'lā* (87) to *Sūrah al-Layl* (92):** These six *sūrahs* focus on *tazkiyah nafs*, i.e., spiritual and moral development of a person which is the most important concern of the Religion. Salvation is not possible without it.

(III) ***Sūrah Aḍ-Ḍuḥā* (93) to *Sūrah al-Bayyinah* (98)**: These six *sūrahs* are concerned with The Revealed Divine Guidance. The Book and the Prophet are the most significant blessings of God to humanity. They contain the path of guidance and help our *tazkiyah* - thereby leading to *Falaḥ*

(IV) ***Sūrah az-Zalzalah* (99) to *Sūrah al-Humazah* (104):** Having discussed the subject of *tazkiyah* (spiritual and moral development of persons) and the subject of Divine Guidance to human life in a dozen *sūrahs*, in the following six *sūrahs* the focus turns to *Ākhirah* (the Hereafter). The issue of 'salvation' and the issue of 'accountability' are closely related with 'the life after death'. These *sūrahs* make it clear that the fate of the loyal and dutiful servants of God will be different from the fate of the thankless people who are concerned only with immediate pleasures of this life and who thereby fail their test from God.

(V) ***Sūrah al-Fīl* (105) to *Sūrah an-Nās* (114)**: In this last section, The Divine Book makes concluding remarks through ten brief discourses (*sūrahs*), summarizing its most important concerns.

Let us briefly explain the above.

(I) *Sūrah al-Burūj* (85) and *Sūrah aṭ-Ṭāriq* (86)

Sūrah al-Burūj (85) removes the misapprehension in some minds that a law of the jungle operates in the human world. The unjust corrupt powers consider that they can continue their persecution of innocent believers and God will not take any action against them. *Sūrah aṭ-Ṭāriq* (86) clarifies: these unjust persecutors do not know that God, Who is well aware of their hidden plots against the Prophet and his followers, already has a Divine plot against them, ready to operate. However, The Wise and The Merciful God is still giving some time to to God's disobedient servants so that they make *tawbah* (repentance) and seek God's forgiveness, before God's Punishment arrives.

This section gives assurance of Divine help to the believers. *Sūrah al-Burūj* (85) and *Sūrah aṭ-Ṭāriq* (86) together aim at giving the believers consolation and encouragement. **Thus these two Divine discourses prepare the minds of the beleving readers for a study of the following twenty eight *sūrahs*, with greater peace of mind.**

(II)*Sūrah al-A'lā* (87) to *al-Layl* (92): *Tazkiyah*: Nature, Significance

This section focuses on *tazkiyah* (spiritual and moral development) of *nafs* (of a person) or even that of a whole community of persons. *Tazkiyah* being the most important concern of the Religion (*ad-Dīn*), *Sūrah al-A'lā* (87) is the first *lesson* to the Prophet from his *Rabb* (Lord). *Sūrah al-A'lā* (87) explains that the whole creation is glorifying the Creator. The Prophet also should prostrate to God and glorify God, The Most High. Through the Qur'an, the Prophet shall awaken his addressees to the remembrance (*dhikr*) of God. If he sees that his reminding the people is working, he should further take care of their *tazkiyah* (spiritual and moral progress). The Salvation and Ultimate Happiness and Success (*Al-Falāḥ*) lies in spiritual and moral development (*tazkiyah).* However, due to their love of immediate pleasures the people develop forgetfulness and do not care for their own moral and spiritual progress. Earlier Divine scriptures clearly explained this point.

It is in this perspective that *Sūrah al-Ghāshiyah* (88) deals at length with *Khusrān* (Doom) and *Falāḥ*. It is not without reason that *Sūrah al-Ghāshiyah* (88) underlines the point of *fikr* (reflecting and pondering over the signs of God). This point was implicit in *Sūrah al-A'lā* (87), which underlined the point of *dhikr* (remembrance of God).

The following four *sūrahs* further develop the composite theme which the above couple of Divine discourses make together. Just consider: *Sūrah al-Fajr* (89) underlines the significance of those calm and quiet moments which the believers use for *fikr*, e.g., reflection on one's own life, and *dhikr,* e.g., remembrance of God's name or listening to the recitation of *KalāmAllāh,* The Divine Speech or the Qur'an. The people who totally neglect such remembrance and reflection get lost in lower pursuits. They develop transgression against God. This leads to mutual exploitation and thereby fills the earth with corruption. This is exactly what happened with the People of 'Ād, People of Thamūd and the People of Pharaoh. The prophets of God reminded them of their duty to their Creator and their fellow servants. They called them to contemplate what was wrong with their lives. But these people would not listen. If today's transgressors will also turn a deaf ear to the call of the Prophet of God, their fate will not be different from earlier transgressors who were punished by God here in this life and who will enter the Hell in the Hereafter. The *sūrah* implicitly suggests that due to their lack of remembrance of God these people have no inner peace even in this life.

On the other hand, the believers who do not neglect their duty to their fellow human beings, enjoy perfect inner peace through remembrance of God, even here in the present phase of life. However, in the Hereafter, these virtuous people will be in the Vicinity of God and they will enjoy the company of God's virtuous servants in Paradise.

Sūrah al-Balad (90) which underlines that by their very nature human beings are very hard working, explicitly deals with another aspect of *tazkiyah* i.e. practically striving in the way of our social obligations., e.g. working for the elimination of all kinds of slavery and sharing in the needs of our fellow human beings. It emphasizes our concern with the deprived and alienated sections of human society.

Sūrah al-Balad also introduces the role of the Qur'anic Movement (90:17) as a collective striving of the virtuous people, which is inviting all conscientious people to join.

Sūrah al-Shams (91) and the *Sūrah al-Layl* (92) together, further elaborate the above role of the Qur'anic Movement. Both use the metaphor of sun for the enlightenment which the Book brings. They both explain: those who take care of their *tazkiyah* benefit from the Divine Guidance just like day which shines in the light of sun. On the other hand those who are unconcerned with their *tazkiyah* act like an opaque medium. Their example is that of night because they cover the light of Divine Guidance.

(As we notice, the first *sūrah, i.e., Sūrah aḍ- Ḍuḥā* (93) of the next section, begins with the good news: *Day is coming* and Light will spread everywhere. All darkness will go away. This *sūrah* also uses the same metaphor.)

(III) *Sūrah aḍ- Ḍuḥā* (93) to *Sūrah al-Bayyinah* (98)

The Prophet & the Prophetic Job: Revealed Guidance in Human Life: The above section has already prepared the ground for this section. These six *sūrahs* show how Reveled Divine Guidance is related to human life. The Book and the Prophet are viewed as the most significant blessings of God to humanity. *Sūrah aḍ- Ḍuḥā* (93) and *Sūrah Ash-Sharḥ* (94) have their focus on the personality of the Prophet. They deal with the special relationship of this *very special servant of God* with his Lord. Through setting his own example of thanksgiving, the Prophet teaches others how to lead their lives as God's thankful servants. While *Sūrah aḍ-Ḍuḥā* (93) briefly introduces what is involved in the Prophetic job, *Sūrah Ash-Sharḥ* (94) explains how this job will become easier for him. The two Divine discourses prepare the ground for *Sūrah at-Tīn* (95) and *Sūrah al-'Alaq* (96).

Sūrah at-Tīn (95) introduces the Prophetic Movement, in the historical perspective of Jesus, Moses and Abraham, while *Sūrah al-'Alaq* (96) initiates the Prophetic Movement in the concrete human situation which the Prophet encounters. He does so by way of reading the Book to his addressees and leading his movement, courageously and wisely, in the light of the Book.

Sūrah al-Qadr (97) points out: the angels of God, under the leadership of the Spirit of The Holy (The Archangel Gabriel) will descend every year during The Night of *al-Qadr or the night when the Qur'an was first sent down. They will bring all kinds of Divine blessings to the human world.* (These are, in fact, fruits of the Qur'anic Movement.) This suggests that believers should devote this night to remembrance of God and recitation and contemplation over Divine Signs. *Sūrah al-Qadr* (97) establishes the relevance of the Qur'anic Movement for future human situations.

Sūrah al-Bayyinah (98), on the other hand, introduces *the point of realism in order* that the believers do not develop any frustration. The *sūrah* explains that all those who stand in the way of the Qur'anic Movement are not innocently ignorant of the Truth. It is true mainly of the two groups that this *sūrah* mentions. The way God has made things clear to these two groups, no doubt is possible in the authenticity of the Book or the Prophet. Likewise, the *tawḥīdic* message of the Qur'an is perfectly clear - as was, earlier, the case with Torah. Therefore, the unjust disbelievers deserve Divine Punishment. On the other hand, the virtuous believers, who are leading the *īmānic* movement, in spite of the difficult situation created by their opponents, will be highly honored by their Forgiving and Merciful Lord.

(IV) *Sūrah az-Zalzalah* (99) to *Sūrah al-Humazah* (104)

The Hereafter and the Way to 'Salvation' or '*al-Falāḥ*'

The following six *sūrahs* bring the focus on 'what human beings will ultimately receive in the life after their death as a reward of their striving in the present phase of life.' In order to understand the system that underlies the arrangement of these six *sūrahs*, we will further divide this section into two subsections as follows:

(IV) A consists of two pairs

Sūrah az-Zalzalah (99) - *Sūrah al-'Ādiyāt* (100) and *Sūrah al-Qāri'ah* (101) - *Sūrah at-Takāthur* (102)

Consider the first *sūrah* of each pair. Both *Sūrah az-Zalzalah* and *Sūrah al-Qāri'ah* use two different styles to divert readers' attention to the great catastrophe that will initiate an altogether new world order. However, the emphasis in *az-Zalzalah* is on **seeing**. Everyone shall see what one did in this life even if it is a virtuous deed of the size of an atom or an evil deed of similar size. The Earth itself will relate the whole story of the performance of humankind. On the other hand, *Sūrah al-Qāri'ah* underlines weightlessness or weightfulness of human actions: objects which seem to possess great *weight* in this phase of life will lose all their weight on that day. Good deeds alone will carry weight. However, in each of the two pairs of *sūrahs* (99-100 and 101-102), the second *sūrah* goes deeper into the perspective. According to *Sūrah al-'Ādiyāt* (100), the most basic evil is the ingratitude of human beings. However, it is their love of wealth which causes this forgetfulness. This love of wealth is strengthened by their neglect of *Ākhirah. Sūrah at-Takāthur* (102) goes further: the people who are lost in the pursuit of worldly gains try to surpass each other in having more and better material gains and they are *so lost in this race* that they do not have any time left to give their thanks to God or even think of it. They totally forget that through these blessings God is testing them and that on the Judgment Day they will have to account for 'how they manipulated these resources?'

(IV) B consists of one pair

***Sūrah al-'Aṣr* (1 03) and *Sūrah al-Humazah* (104)**

This last section directly addresses the subject of Salvation (*al- Falāḥ)* and Doom (*al-Khusrān*).

Sūrah al-'Aṣr (103) draws a lesson from the history of the prophetic movement. The humankind is rushing towards its doom – closing its eyes to what happened with ancient civilizations that rejected the message of the prophets of God. The *sūrah* suggests the following four points for the achievement of *Falāḥ*:

1. Believing is joining this *īmānic* movement. Respond to the call of the prophets of God. Come out of the servitude of other than One God.

2. Follow the path of virtue - mutual concern and mutual respect.

3. Encourage each other in the performance of our mutual duties.

4. Give moral support to each other, mainly when we face difficult situations.

However, *Sūrah al-Humazah* (104), which is concerned with the root cause, goes deeper into the understanding of the rotten mentality of a corrupt worshipper of wealth whose heart is full of hate for his/her fellow humans. This individual flares the Anger of The Merciful God and is, therefore, responsible for his/her own doom. Unlike the worshiper of One God who walks in the Light of God (*NūrAllāh*) and has perfect peace of mind, this niggardly worshipper of wealth chose Fire of God (*NārAllāh*).

(V) *Sūrah al-Fīl* (105) – *Sūrah an-Nās* (114)

The Divine Book makes its concluding remarks, summarizing the most important Divine concerns.

This last section comprises four pairs of sūrahs and two single *sūrahs* – in all, ten *sūrahs*. Thus it can be further divided into six subsections. **Consider subsections (a) to (f) in the following.**

a) ***Both Sūrah al-Fīl* (105) and *Sūrah al-Quraysh* (106)** underline the significance of the House of God in Makkah as the center of Global Qur'anic Movement. However, they have roles which are complimentary to each other.

The *Sūrah al-Fīl* brings us back to a theme similar to that of *Sūrah al-Burūj* (85) and *Sūrah at-Ṭāriq* (86), from where we started in this brief study of Qur'anic *sūrahs*. In *Sūrah al-Fīl* (105) also, the address is directly to the Prophet and indirectly to all the believers. The Prophet should continue his job with perfect peace of mind. God will protect the *Tawḥīdic* Movement and its International Spiritual Center. The Prophet need not worry.

In *Sūrah Quraysh* (106), the address is to the Children of Ishmael who reside in the vicinity of the House of God. God fulfilled the promise (2:126) to Ishmael and his father Abraham, concerning the security and sustenance to those who would reside in the neighborhood of The House of God. Now, these neighbors of the House of God should also do their part as worshippers of One God alone. They should stand up in support of the *tawḥīdic* mission of Abraham, which is now being revived by the Prophet.

b) ***Sūrah al-Mā'ūn* (107) and *Sūrah al-Kawthar* (108)** deal with the nature and the fate of false religiosity and true religiosity. *Sūrah al-Mā'ūn* remarks, the opponents of the Qur'anic Movement are, in fact, representatives of false religiosity. They have stood in opposition to the Qur'anic Movement because it is reviving the true religiosity which emphasizes human concerns and commands that the sincere worshippers of God take care of their social obligations which are, in fact, assignments from their Lord.

According to *Sūrah al-Kawthar* (108), the religiosity to which the Qur'an is calling has two components: prayer (*ṣalāh)* and sacrifice. The first one involves submisson to God throughout one's life and standing in the presence of God in prayer, while the latter symbolizes believers' encounter of all kinds of difficulties, in God's way. And it includes sharing in the needs of our fellow human beings to gain God's pleasure.

False religiosity is showy - even so in its (traditional) prayers. True religiosity lies in experiencing Divine Presence as one stands before God, bows down and prostrates to God. Practitioners of false religiosity have no concern with the needs of others while a truly religious person seeks Divine pleasure through doing his/her duty assigned from God (e.g.) concerning downtrodden and alienated people. *Sūrah al-Kawthar* underlines prayer (*ṣalāh*) and sacrifice as its two basic components. As the believing community proceeds, taking care of both of these, the blessing of the Qur'an go on increasing. Ultimately, true religiosity prevails and false religiosity withers away.

c) ***Sūrah al-Kāfirūn*** **(109)** proclaims the Qur'anic policy on Freedom of Religion: Everyone is free to choose one's religion out of one's own free will. Therefore, no external pressure is justified by any party. The Qur'anic Movement declares that it does not believe in making partners with One God. It is not going to submit to any external pressure to make any *compromise in its tawḥīdic message.*

d) ***Sūrah An-Naṣr*** **(110) and** ***Sūrah al-Masad*** **(111):**

Sūrah An-Naṣr **(110):** Divine Help will bring Victory of the Qur'anic Movement, thus making the above freedom available, for large crowds of people, to enter into the Religion of God. Therefore, *Sūrah An-Naṣr* (110) comes back to the same reminder with which *Sūrah al-A'lā* (87) started. However, 'in gratitude' which was implicit in *Sūrah al-'A'lā*(87) is also made explicit in *An-Naṣr*. This time it also adds '*seeking God's forgiveness and returning to God'* to 'making *tasbīḥ* or glorifying God, in gratitude.' We should not forget that the victory is achieved in spite of our shortcoming.

Sūrah al-Masad **(111):** This *sūrah* deals with the fate of pseudo-religiosity. Here, we have a lover of wealth, who is totally devoid of all human concerns - a person wearing a false garb of spirituality. This character fits very well with the one dealt with in *Sūrah al-Mā'ūn* (107).

e) ***Sūrah al-Ikhlāṣ*** **(112):** At the very end of the Book the Prophet is told to make a clear and courageous statement that no one is worthy of worship but One

God. God has no duality and no plurality in God's Being. God is just One! All beings depend upon God. God does not depend on any other being. No one is like God.

Before we close our reading of the Book, **we seek God's protection in the following two *sūrahs*.**

f) ***Sūrah al-Falaq* (113) & *Sūrah an-Nās* (114):** Coming of the Light of Guidance threatens worshipers of darkness. Satan, the Great Envier is frustrated as the Qur'anic Movement succeeds in bringing the people back to the message of earlier prophets of God, and human kind is on its way to become one family of God's servants again.

The Qur'anic Movement faces many challenges. The last two *sūrahs* underline: Do not fear. Do not worry. Seek God's refuge. Act rationally and firmly. Do not entertain satanic instigations and irrational doubts. God is the Creator of all beings. God alone is the Lord, the King and the Deity of all humans. God is with you. Ultimately, Divine light will spread everywhere.

Glossary

The Book	The Qur'an uses 'the Book' for various Divine books revealed to various messengers - treating these books as different editions of the same Divine Book, and treating the Qur'an as its final edition.
The Guidance	Unlike 'guidance,', 'the Guidance' is used for Revealed Guidance in Divine Words or 'the Book.'
The Messenger	Unlike 'the messenger' or 'the prophet' which is general,
The Prophet	'the Prophet' or 'the Messenger' is used for Muhammad, the last and the final Prophet and Messenger of God.
The Religion	'The Religion' stands for Qur'anic 'ad-*Dīn'* or the religion of the prophets of God - including Muhammad. Abraham was the first person to name it 'al-Islām.' Thus the Religion is one; the religions are many.
Servant	As a Qur'anic term servant stands for *'abd.* *'Rabb* - *'abd'* stands for God - human relation.
Sūrah	The Qur'an is composed of 114 discourses or *sūrahs*. These are composed of *āyāt* (signs). Every *āyah* makes a point.
Tauhid	Coming out of the serritude of other than God and becoming servant of One God alone.

* also have a look at Quranic termsexplained in Chapter Two.

Index